WHEN MORE IS NOT ENOUGH

How to Stop Giving Your Kids
What They Want
and Give Them What They Need

Amy L. Sullivan

Lighthouse Publishing
of the Carolinas

www.lighthousepublishingofthecarolinas.com

WHEN MORE IS NOT ENOUGH: HOW TO STOP GIVING YOUR KIDS WHAT THEY WANT AND GIVE THEM WHAT THEY NEED BY AMY L. SULLIVAN
Published by Lighthouse Publishing of the Carolinas
2333 Barton Oaks Dr., Raleigh, NC, 27614

ISBN 978-1-941103-24-1
Copyright © 2014 by Amy L. Sullivan
Cover design by writelydesigned.com
Interior design by Karthick Srinivasan

Available in print from your local bookstore, online, or from the publisher at:
www.lighthousepublishingofthecarolinas.com

For more information on this book and the author visit: AmyLSullivan.com

Brought to you by the creative team at LighthousePublishingoftheCarolinas.com: Alycia W. Morales, Michele Creech, Rowena Kuo, Cindy Sproles, Brian Cross, and Eddie Jones.

Library of Congress Cataloging-in-Publication Data
Sullivan, Amy L.
When More is Not Enough: How to Stop Giving Your Kids What They Want and Give Them What They Need/ Amy L. Sullivan, 1st ed.

Printed in the United States of America

Praise For *When More is Not Enough*

With a voice that's funny, quirky and real, author Amy L. Sullivan shares her own family's struggles with egocentricity and entitlement and how they moved from abundant stuff to an abundant life of serving others. *When More is Not Enough* is a must-read for young and old alike, but especially for parents longing to rescue their children—and themselves—from the prowling beast of narcissism.

~ Renae Brumbaugh
Best-selling author and award-winning humor columnist

In *When More is Not Enough*, Amy L. Sullivan will have your whole family doing heart checks around the kitchen table. She will take you through the journey of moving from self-focused to others-focused, all while keeping it real with her fun and engaging style. A must-read for any family desiring direction and motivation to change the me-centered generations found in their very own home.

~ Kristen Summers
Author of *Teach Me to Serve, 99 Ways Preschoolers Can Learn to Serve and Bless Others*

The epidemic of families and children with self-obsessed attitudes has risen to a near crisis. Families have been lulled into comfort and complacency as they quietly build their American Dream all the while asking, "What's missing?" Amy not only puts a finger on the very thing we can't quite name but also takes us by the hand and guides us to "other-centered living." She opens our eyes to living outside ourselves through a servant's heart. *When More is Not Enough* will ignite a passion within your family to open the doors and serve others.

~ Heather Riggleman
Author of *Mama Needs a Time Out*
Blogger at The Real Mom, heatherriggleman.com

When More is Not Enough by Amy L. Sullivan is an essential book for parents wanting to raise generous children (and become more generous themselves). Each chapter contains practical ways families can serve: in their homes, in their communities, and in the world. Plus, at the end of each chapter is a section called Dinner Table Dialogue. These questions are a great way to get the entire family thinking about how to live more generously. Amy's conversational, down-to-earth style will encourage you to make changes toward generous living without making you feel guilty in the process.

~ Lindsey Bell
Author of *Searching for Sanity: 52 Insights from the Parents of the Bible*

CONTENTS

ADDITIONAL RESOURCES:

ACKNOWLEDGEMENTS

I need to acknowledge those who made the work you are holding happen.

Jesus,
Walking into churches used to make me uncomfortable, itchy, and hot. How did I end up writing a book that will be shelved in the Christian nonfiction section? I think I may hear You laughing.

Shane, Amelia, and Ruby,
This book is as much yours as it is mine. You are the exact family I always hoped for. I love you more than crackling campfires and the Colorado sky.

Lori,
We were writers since our first issue of the *Treasure Island Trailer Park Times*. Thanks for cheering longer and harder than anyone.

Denise,
I know you want to remain anonymous, and therefore, I won't tell others how you contributed to this book. Instead, I will use a special made-up word, which rhymes with the actual way in which you helped me. Don't worry. I am certain readers will not pick up on this. Thank you for "fediting" my initial manuscript.

To GFN, I think the best stories start in a blizzard with an old Jeep Cherokee, a rickety U-Haul, and a handmade coffee table.

INTRODUCTION

When God said to love one another as He has loved us (John13:34-35), I'm pretty sure He meant it. That's it. That's the entire introduction. Actually, that's the entire book. Close the cover and act upon this wisdom.

Just kidding … sort of.

THE REST OF THE INTRODUCTION

I'm glad you are here. And as my husband would say, hunker down.

This book is for you, but it's also for me.

Oh, who am I kidding? This book is mostly for me, and if you can glean a bit from the pages of our middle-class family's struggle to beat down entitlement by serving others, well, that makes me I-can't-get-this-ridiculous-smile-off-my-face happy.

Many of you do an amazing job of serving others. A servant's heart grew in you long ago, and doing for others comes naturally. You jump at the chance to make a meal or make a friend or make a difference. For this, I applaud you. Selflessness doesn't come easy for me.

This book explains what happens when a doted-upon Pentecostal preacher's kid marries an if-you-want-it-you-better-work-for-it Catholic girl. Quick summary: You get a couple—and eventually a family—who unintentionally gobbles up all life offers.

Hi, I'm Amy, the "if-you-want-it-you-better-work-for-it" girl in the story. Life was cruising along smoothly until one day, the dense fog of my self-absorbed world lifted. My eyes refocused, and I looked around and observed selfishness. I saw a world consumed by the hottest must-have tech gadget, the next soccer trophy, and the shelves full of photos of smiling people on sandy beaches.

Our family's constant chase after temporal things exhausted me and seemed pointless. Why did cool phones, plastic awards, and sunny getaways matter? Truth was, they didn't, and I hated my constant pursuit of them.

This book grew out of a past Christmas experience. I wish I could say our daughters tore the Christmas wrap off their gifts and then stomped and pouted because they wanted more gifts. But sadly, the foot stomping and pouting came from the adults in the story: my husband and I.

Two days after Christmas, my husband and I wanted to spend a little money. As if the typical holiday gifting wasn't enough, we investigated all the post-Christmas sales eager to use the gift cards and cash that filled our pockets. Something about our endless spending seemed wrong, but we rationalized our splurging. We weren't actually using *our* hard-earned money; we were simply spending the money we received as gifts. The case was easy to justify.

A new North Face jacket—check. A new set of Polly Pockets—check. More Christmas candy—check. An Atlanta Braves baseball hat—check.

Walking past an artsy store, we noticed a framed picture of the word *FAMILY*. This was different from anything we had seen before because each letter of the word *FAMILY* was a photograph of a real-life object representing the letter. The *F* was a sideways view of a stoplight. The *A* was an arch in a building. The *M* was an iron curve of a bicycle rack, and so on. Inside the artsy store, a big box of photo letters invited us to spell anything we wanted. Great idea. Again, something we must have.

Shane and I brainstormed words which represented our family. We wanted something original. Something beyond the normal "Live, Laugh, Love" idea, but what?

"Ours," Shane suggested.

"Ours," I whispered back. Perfect.

Of course, "ours" fit us. Our house. Our cars. Our clothes. Our vacations. Our church. Our kids. Our desires and our endless list of wants.

We bought the photographs, and not long after, I framed them. You heard me. We framed the word *OURS*.

As I stood admiring my new piece of art, God whispered, "Yes, all of this is yours, and that is a problem. What is mine in your life?"

His? I paused, convicted.

Nothing was His. Like a two-year-old on a bad play date, I envisioned myself with arms flailing, grabbing everything within my reach and shrieking at the thought of anyone touching my things.

Days passed, and I realized it was more than just our must-have attitudes that bothered me. Over time, materialism slinked into our hearts, and mindless busyness filled our hours. We did virtually nothing for others. God sacrificed his Son for us, but we sacrificed little for anyone.

I defended our behavior in my head.

We work hard. We save money. We pay bills. Our bank accounts aren't bursting. We are straight-up middle class. Why shouldn't we buy what we want?

Plus, we acknowledge the needs of others. Sometimes. Kind of.

We support a little girl in Africa. We save money to give our babysitter at the end of the year. We spend extra time with that hurting family.

But even after I credited the invisible "good deeds account" in my head, every act of generosity committed by our family over the last year fell short. Way short.

God wanted more. He expected it. God desired to take what we saw as ours and turn it into His. He wanted us to teach our kids to live an entitled-free lifestyle, but first He wanted us to live it.

It was time to show our love for God by demonstrating our love for people (Matthew 22:37-38).

So, my husband and I reluctantly agreed. We decided our family would no longer strive for the next big thing. Instead, we would strive for the Real Thing (translation: God), but how?

We had no idea, but we knew the Real Thing required our

family to take the focus off ourselves and concentrate on the needs of others. God wanted us to stop consuming and start serving.

This idea did not excite me.

How could we go from obsessing over the paint color in our spare room to living a life devoted to others? Could we find a way to fight our self-obsessed attitudes? Would God require us to do more than write a tiny check to a cause we only half-heartedly cared about? Please, God, no. Would we have to move to the mission field or adopt a child? That's what the big givers do, you know.

I thought of service as a series of tasks.

I also thought serving others meant our family would fly to Africa to dig wells, rescue orphans, or perhaps do something involving mosquito nets.

But then, I started to get the feeling God didn't want across-the-ocean acts of service from us (at least not yet). Instead, He wanted us to move in our community (yawn). He wanted our family to shake off comfortable and start to act.

And I think He desires the same thing from all of us.

Yes, you. And me.

The ones who aren't sure why we picked up this book but who are very certain of the dozens of reasons we can't find a way for our families to serve others—at least not right now.

We're hurting. We're broke. We're broken. We don't have time. We don't have energy. We're too busy. We don't have an area of expertise. We don't need something else to juggle. And, oh yeah, we don't have anything to give.

In 2 Corinthians 8:12, Paul states, *For if the willingness is there, the gift is acceptable according to what one has, not according to what he does not have.*

That's all. We just need a willingness to give, nothing else. Let's talk.

Giving advice on how to raise others-centered kids is not me. I know we just met, but trust me on this one. First, what do I know? Second, if seeing and meeting the needs of others doesn't come naturally to me, doling out guidance to others on giving seems wrong.

So instead of advice, I want to share from one mom to another what our beyond-blessed family learned when we opened our eyes to the needs surrounding us. However, I don't want you to think of the ideas here as a magical formula to fix yourself and your kids. Heck, no.

As you read, you will notice only a few references to my husband. Please don't take this to mean he wasn't involved. In fact, it was Shane who continuously stated, "For this to work, we have to do it together." When I wanted to dart ahead and make quick changes, he reminded me that lasting change is never quick.

Plus, Shane allowed me to use his famous "hunker down" phrase, and he also penned a letter to all the dads in the house. You will find his letter and other valuable resources in the back of the book.

Actually, now is the perfect time to talk about the resources in the back of the book. In addition to the letter from my husband, *To a Dad from a Dad,* there is also *Books that Inspire Action,* which is a comprehensive list of books for children and adults regarding others-centered living.

After this, you will find *Clickity, Click*, which lists a slew of family-friendly websites to help readers kick-start service. And to support chapter seven on being generous with your time, you will find a letter entitled *Dear Parents* that was written by our ten-year-old daughter.

I'm telling you all of this now because this book is different, and you don't need to read it cover to cover. *Say what?* Your high school English teacher would fall over. Each chapter discusses a topic and ways your family can serve others by being generous in a particular area. Skip around and discover what suits you; the chapters stand alone.

My hope is that you drag this book to the dinner table and discuss it with your family. Then, you accidently spill spaghetti sauce on it. You take it to your favorite lunch spot, and after lunch, you forget the book in your car. It bounces around and the cover gets beat up, but then you remember it's in your car and give it to a friend. Your friend takes it to the beach, and it gets sandy. Your friend gives it to her sister who carts it to her office to look up the online resources, and she spills coffee on it.

I've said all this to say I want you to use this book. If I walk into your house and find it in perfect condition on the top shelf, I know it will not have accomplished what I set out for it to do: be a resource on growing giving hearts.

Write all over the pages. Highlight this bad boy right up. Interacting and underlining is permitted and encouraged.

That's enough yammering. It's time to dive in and talk about the beast of entitlement, the one we helped to create in our kids. I know I said skipping around in this book is permitted, but you are not allowed to skip the next section. It's a rule, kind of like a law.

And while we are talking about laws, there is one more. Guilt keeps no space here. No. This book is a guilt-free zone.

When I first told a friend about this book, she said, "I think it's a good idea, but promise me you won't make readers feel guilty. No one really changes because of guilt. Inspire readers. Help us get excited about serving."

I hope I've kept my promise.

CHAPTER 1

BATTLING THE BEAST
WE HELPED CREATE
We Did This

Get back, you ugly thing, and take your iPod, Kindle, five American Girl dolls, and castle-like play set with you!

I'm not sure when I saw youth entitlement strut across my life and shake its tiny fist at me.

Maybe it was at my co-worker's house when a hardworking, middle-class grandma asked her granddaughter to pick up the toys, which lined the floor of her living room, and the girl snapped, "You pick it up. You are the one who bought me all this stuff!"

Or it could have been when I asked a room full of high school students what chores they were responsible for and only two students admitted to having responsibilities around the house.

Perhaps it was the parade of tasteless T-shirts, sported by toddlers and teens alike, shouting words and phrases such as "Princess" and "Diva" and "I'm in charge."

It could have been the family who decided renting ponies at their child's over-the-top birthday party wasn't enough, so they hired someone to paint the ponies pink for the day.

Maybe it's the fact that after fourteen years in education, the number of kids I see suffering from anxiety, depression, and stress-related ailments has never been higher.

Or it could be the heaps of books published over the last ten years warning us about the current path of our parenting. Pick up the *Price of Privilege: How Parental Pressure and Material Advantage are Creating a Generation of Disconnected and Unhappy Kids* by Madeline Levine. Peruse *The Narcissism Epidemic: Living in the Age of Entitlement* by Jean M. Twenge and W. Keith Campbell. Skim *Generation Me: Why Today's Americans Are More Confident, Assertive, Entitled, and more Miserable Than Ever Before* by Jean M. Twenge. Each book paints a picture of a generation of weak and coddled kids.

Initially, I thought youth entitlement a problem for the overly indulged, but when I spend time with kids of different socioeconomic backgrounds, I observe this same sense of entitlement attacking kids from all ranks of society.

Take, for example, a homeless high school junior I used to teach. I took him to an orientation at an institution offering free, post-secondary training and free housing for at-risk teens, and he deemed the program inappropriate because he was going to be a millionaire. Then, he asked me for lunch money and a ride.

Whatever it was, one thing is clear: Entitlement in our youth is running like wild Kudzu in the South, strangling the life out of everything it crosses, and entitlement in our youth is our fault.

Yes, our fault. Yours and mine.

Parenting Then and Now

In the book, *Narcissism Epidemic*, authors Jean M. Twenge and W. Keith Campbell state that today, more than any other time in history, parents put children's needs first.[1]

My Grandpa Bud and my father never spoke of life after high school, and with his high school career ending, my father approached my grandfather for fatherly direction and advice.

What should he do after high school?

Without looking up from his work, my grandfather responded. "You have three options: Get a job. Go to college. Or join the military."

End of conversation.

This hands-off attitude is a stark contrast to parental involvement in the lives of children today.

Not only do we pour over decisions regarding preschools, healthy food choices, and play groups, but our heavy parental involvement doesn't end at the preschool doors. It continues through college and beyond.

Some say this is good. Our kids feel loved and supported. Others say helicopter parenting is turning our kids into the overly needy who require constant encouragement and support.

In a recent *USA Today* article, Paul Davidson tells the astonishing account of a man in his late twenties who brought his father with him for a forty-five minute job interview.[2] Can you imagine? Nothing says you can count on me like your father urging you on from the next seat over.

With the idea of being active, caring, and involved parents, we have placed our children at the center of our universe. Why wouldn't our kids think the world belongs to them?

It's easy to look around and place blame on what is now dubbed "iGeneration" or "Generation Me" on reality television, poor role models, helicopter parenting, playgrounds with recycled rubber floors, video games, lowered standards, sanitized living, and working families.

And that is all true. Countless areas of childrearing need to be rethought, retaught, and revamped.

Yeah, Yeah, Yeah, but Now What?

This isn't just another book to tell you what a helpless mess our kids are turning out to be. Nope, this book examines one simple idea that has the potential to save our youth from the weak generation many have deemed them to be: generous living.

To purge the attitude of youth entitlement, we need to teach our kids to serve others. But, to teach our kids to serve others, we must first look at our attitude toward serving. If our families are to understand self-worth isn't tied to the world's standards

(Luke 16:14c), we need to implement changes in our own lives, and quickly.

Ha! You didn't see that one coming, did you? You thought this little paperback gave you step-by-step instructions on how to change those unruly kids of yours.

I tricked you. (Insert loud laugher and envision me tossing my head back and rubbing my hands together.)

Consider the Following:

- Jessica Ekstrom, a nineteen-year-old intern from North Carolina, pulls her hair into a ponytail and can't stop thinking about girls with cancer who lose their hair during chemotherapy. Jessica worries about how cancer impacts a young girl's self-esteem and creates Headbands of Hope, an organization dedicated to fighting childhood cancer and helping girls feel beautiful by giving them sassy and stylish headbands.
- Sisters Delaney (age 9) and Addie (age 8) Kenney decide to hold an Almost Sleepover and collect pajamas for local kids in need. In doing so, they inspire over 1,200 girls from 26 states to hold Almost Sleepovers of their own, impacting over 100 charities nationwide.
- When ten-year-old Reshini Premaratne was told she was too young to volunteer, she could have given up. Instead, she founded X-Out Homelessness, a youth-led service campaign which impacted over 10,000 students and raised over 275 pounds of goods for the homeless in her community.[3]

These stories of young people seeing a need and acting on it fill me with hope and assurance that we aren't going to lose our kids to themselves.

Instead, we will help our children and ourselves see the needs of others. And when we do, the unrelenting pull to the mirror, life attached to the nearest screen, and the chase for stuff will lessen.

It's Survey Time!

Grab a pencil.

On the following pages, you will find three versions of the same inventory: adult, tween/teen, and child. Each question correlates with a corresponding chapter (except the child version, which is modified) in this book. If you need more space for your kiddos to take the inventory, grab some blank paper.

Ready? Go ahead, flip the page.

Let's get this party started.

Service Inventory
Adult

1. **Entitled behavior in our house is**
   a. Minimal
   b. No worse than in the home of others
   c. Bordering out of control

   Ways I serve my family are:

   _____
   _____
   _____
   _____

   Ways I serve my community are:

   _____
   _____
   _____
   _____

   Ways I serve the world are:

   _____
   _____
   _____
   _____

2. **I discuss the needs of others with my children on a regular basis, and by "regular" I mean:**
   a. Daily
   b. Weekly
   c. Monthly

3. **Four skills and talents I possess:**

   _____
   _____
   _____
   _____

4. **I know someone who doesn't have enough to eat.**
   a. Yes. _____ (write a name)
   b. Nope.

5. **I pray for these people on a regular basis:**

   _____
   _____
   _____
   _____

6. **When I am wronged or betrayed by someone:**
   a. I feel hurt. But, in time, I find a way to forgive.
   b. I hold a grudge for some time and then forgive, but not happily.
   c. I don't forgive. I believe if someone hurts me once, they will do it again.

7. **I enjoy writing checks to support causes I feel strongly about.**
   a. My checkbook is always open.
   b. I give when I have money to give.
   c. You are kidding me, right?

8. **How do you protect your family's time?**

   _____
   _____
   _____
   _____

9. **When I hear about _____ on the news, it bothers me. Often I think about it later in the day or during the week.**

Service Inventory
Tween/Teen
(Ages 8-18)

1. Do you usually get what you want? Think of a recent time when you didn't get what you hoped for. How did you handle it?

_____

_____

_____

_____

2. List two ways your family helps others.

_____

_____

_____

_____

3. List four skills or talents you have.

_____

_____

_____

_____

4. Do you know anyone who doesn't have enough to eat? Who?

_____

_____

_____

_____

5. Who do you pray for?

_____

_____

_____

_____

6. **Do you forgive easily or do you hold grudges? Discuss a recent conflict and how you handled it.**

_____

_____

_____

_____

7. **What do you usually spend your money on?**

_____

_____

_____

_____

8. **How much time during the week do you spend on the following:**

_____ Watching TV

_____ Playing on the computer

_____ Texting or talking on the phone

_____ Hanging out with friends

9. **When is the last time you saw someone in need of help and wanted to help them?**

_____

_____

_____

_____

Modified Service Inventory
Child (Ages 5-8)

Parents, the child survey is meant to be completed with an adult. Please coach your child through the questions and write down any answers that are too difficult for your kiddo to complete on his or her own.

1. Draw a picture of something you can do to help others.

2. Draw a picture of an activity you know how to do well (Examples: drawing, singing, making friends).

3. Draw a picture of two people you can pray for.

4. When is the last time someone hurt your feelings? What did you do to show them they were forgiven?

    _____
    _____
    _____
    _____

5. **When you receive an allowance or a gift of money, what do you usually spend it on?**

_____

_____

_____

_____

Let's Get Practical

There's only one assignment for this chapter, and it's to discuss your survey answers with each other. That's it. No more. Easy. Find out what the people in your house are thinking about serving others.

CHAPTER 2

BUT I DON'T KNOW ANY POOR PEOPLE

Why You Need to Just Start

Some people think small acts of service equal small results. I think they are wrong.

Alrighty, world, the Sullivans were ready to serve others.

But how? Do we scour nursing homes or head straight to the closest rescue mission? Even searching for a place to start overwhelmed us.

I brainstormed ways our family could serve. I thought about helping others for months but never acted. I prayed for the perfect service opportunity to present itself. You know, a chance to serve in a way in which we worked outdoors, shared little about our faith, and volunteered on a Saturday between the hours of 3:00-5:00 p.m. Even as service opportunities appeared, I deemed most of them unsuitable for a family, and we continued to do nothing.

Then, the mega, billion-dollar, mouse-eared corporation advertised a promotion called "Give a Day, Get a Day." Disney invited families to volunteer one day at a number of non-profit agencies. In return, each family member earned a free pass to Disney World. I jumped at the prospect and began searching a database of local volunteer opportunities.

Endless opportunities appeared: hospital work, Meals on Wheels, river cleanups, daycare positions at shelters, house building, animal loving, smoke prevention instructors, administrative assistants. Still, nothing fit a family with young children.

I continued to scroll down the page, and then Packs for Kids appeared. Children as young as six and their parents helped pack small bags of food for school-aged children. To make this service experience even more appealing, volunteers worked only a two-hour time slot and would still get free Disney passes. Perfect!

I gulped down two cups of coffee and waited for someone to wake up (preferably cheap husband). I could hardly wait to tell him that, before sunrise, I'd saved hundreds of dollars planning a sure-to-be-memorable vacation which would double as our first act of *service* as a family. Instead, our oldest staggered into the kitchen.

Oh well, she'd do.

"Amelia, I signed us up for a really, super-fun activity we can do as a family."

She rubbed her eyes. "What is it?"

"Volunteering at a warehouse to put together bags of food for kids who don't have enough to eat."

Blank stare.

"Doesn't that sound like fun? We are going to help people who don't have enough to eat."

More eye rubbing.

"What do you think?"

"I don't know anyone who doesn't have enough to eat."

I stared at her. Why should that surprise me? Why would my daughter care about kids without anything to eat if she didn't know they existed?

In our sheltered, safe, self-consumed lives, my husband and I neglected to teach our daughter about the millions of people without food. We forgot to tell her about kids at her school without enough to eat. We skipped important conversations about the financial hardships other families face. Focused on building and bettering our lives, we rarely spoke of the needs of others.

My shortcomings made me pause, but it wasn't too late to spin the conversation.

"That's the great part. We help people we don't know, and we do it as a family."

Continued blank stare.

I throw in the truth, the carrot, the incentive, the bribe if you will.

"And for helping these people, we get free passes for our family to go to Disney World! Isn't that awesome?"

No response. What's wrong with this kid? I said Disney, and it didn't trigger sirens and screaming.

Then she sucked in air and let out an enormous sigh.

"When do we have to help?"

"Next Tuesday night. Just for a couple of hours."

She picked at a random string on her pajamas. "Isn't that a school night?"

Why was she thinking about school at a time like this? *Disney, child, Disney.*

"Yeah, it's a school night."

"Well, I guess that's fine, but I don't really know these people."

"Dad and I are going too, and we'll be with you the whole time."

"Do we have any Lucky Charms?" She yawned.

And this is where we started. The place where even free passes to Disney couldn't elicit excitement in serving others.

In addition to placing two cans of soup, three granola bars, and a box of macaroni and cheese in a hundred brown paper bags, our family also spent two hours discussing poverty, child abuse, bullies, and nutrition. Because packing brown bags required little thought, we also laughed at silly jokes, talked in funny accents, and enjoyed the unexpected gift of lingering in each other's company. That's not the point. The point is we left our house specifically to do something for others, and we enjoyed it. We started. We worked beyond step one.

We didn't change, but we acted.

Regardless of the Selfishness of Yesterday, Tomorrow's Promises Are for You

Hoards of shiny do-gooders don't line the pages of the Bible. Instead, real people with real problems fill page after page—people amazingly similar to us. People who committed ultimate wrongs. People God viewed as more than fit to use for His glory.

I love this fact. It makes me feel as if, regardless of my countless mistakes and past transgressions, I have a fighting chance.

And I'm a sucker for stories of redemption.

Tell me about a prostitute in the lineage of Jesus (Matthew 1:5) or about a Christian bounty hunter turned loyal servant of Jesus (Galatians 1:13-16). Tell me about Jesus, who not only chose to hang out with outcasts but actually preferred it (Luke 15:1-3), and my heart beats faster.

While watching the 2010 drama, *The Fighter*, most moviegoers cheer for the main character—professional boxer, Mickey Ward—whose meddling mother and his loser brother, Dickey, only make Mickey's stagnant boxing career worse.

When I watch the movie, I forget about the struggle of the main character and my attention goes straight to the hopeless brother.

Dickey, a drug-addicted, washed-up has-been deserves nothing. He squandered his chance to be a professional fighter. And yet, the entire time Dickey is on the screen, I pull for him to get a break, to see the world anew, to make a change.

It's not stories of the winners who inspire, but stories of those who aren't likely candidates for success and give it a go anyway—people like selfish, selfish us.

On Doing Nothing and Doing Everything

When our family decided to make others a priority, we swung from not doing anything for anyone to doing everything for everyone. In case you don't know, both ways of thinking are equally dangerous.

See, with the first way of thinking, you wait for the perfect opportunity to involve yourself in service (which, by the way, never comes). The latter way of thinking means you involve yourself in activities just to be involved. You are neither invested nor interested, which leaves you overscheduled but far from productive.

CHAPTER 3
WORKING TOWARD A GOAL
Hotdogs and Loud Music Don't Equal Love

I used to think that serving others meant you just needed to get off your couch. Now I think you should go ahead and get off your couch, but while doing so, you also need a goal.

Our church hosted an event one Sunday in which we cancelled the morning service in favor of venturing into our community to "be the church." Groups scattered across our city and engaged in serving the people who lived there.

Best idea ever! Sign us up, immediately.

But for our group of hopeful do-gooders, this meant we gave away free hot dogs and played loud music for people in one of the worst housing developments in our community. Early on a Sunday morning. Without knowing anyone. Without any follow-up planned.

Who wouldn't love a tribe of strangers blaring music and shouting words about Jesus into a crackling microphone? Honestly, if an unexpected mob showed up in my backyard singing and passing out food, I think I'd lock the door and close the blinds.

While there, a posse of ten-year-old boys threw ice at my daughter and her friend. Ice we brought for drinks we brought to go with a lunch we brought.

"Why would you do that?" my daughter asked in her firm-but-on-the-verge-of-tears voice.

"Shut up, or I'm going to punch your teeth out and make them into dentures," the boy sneered back.

"Are you kidding me?" I pounced.

Silence.

Uh-huh. That's right, kids. A mother is present.

More silence. Followed by six sets of little eyes sizing him up. Then, sizing me up. Then, back to him.

It was a showdown, and I was the adult. Therefore, I would win (obvious mistake).

"Why did you bring all of these white people here?" he spat.

All eyes back on me.

Good question.

What were we doing at this housing development, and what were we hoping to accomplish?

I realized hot dogs and loud music don't always translate into love. Our group arrived with good intentions, but we forgot a plan. While you don't need a well-laid-out strategy to serve others, you do need a goal.

What was our family's goal in regard to serving others? What were we good at? What were our kids interested in? What opportunities were available to us?

Um, zero ideas for any of the above.

Therefore, I sought out family-friendly service agencies in our community and signed up. Once a month, we went into our community, met new people, and served others. And guess what we learned?

- How to clean a horse saddle.
- What the word "nonperishable" means.
- Kids get sick—terminally sick.
- All elderly people don't think kids are cute.
- Most elderly people think kids are cute.
- Fabric scissors work better when cutting fabric.
- Nail polish stands are a good way for kids to raise money (At $30.00 an hour, can you say, "Hello career change?").
- Anyone can pull weeds, even four-year-olds.
- How to talk to people who are different from us.

- There are people in our community who don't have food or friends or family.
- Most food banks don't offer fresh fruits or vegetables.
- A ninety-two-year-old woman who traveled the world, worked years for the Red Cross, and knows five languages can teach you things you will never find in books.
- Just because you deem someone in need of help doesn't mean they want it.

But all of the above is far from all. By getting off of our couch, out of our house, and into our community, we also found areas of service each of our family members liked.

The Husband: Service involving physical activities: coaching at-risk kids, river clean-ups, and manual labor tasks.

Me: Service involving women who struggle: women's shelter, mentoring teens and young moms.

Our oldest: Service allowing her to create or help kids: baking cookies, creating crafts or cards, and befriending kids.

Our youngest: Anything, but only for about thirty minutes. *Fine*. Anything, but only for ten minutes.

We weeded out service activities we didn't enjoy. Anything involving crafts was out for my husband. Just ask him about the good time he had cutting plastic shoe patterns out of empty milk cartons. His hatred for crafts is only trumped by his abhorrence of milk.

Once our family understood what we didn't like, finding service opportunities we enjoyed was easy-peasy, and admittedly—wait for it—fun. Okay, we started to have fun.

Caution: Serious Breakthrough Ahead

One night, while volunteering at a home which offers free housing to people with sick relatives, I met a woman. Her daughter lay in a hospital bed less than a mile away. Because of our own experience with a chronically ill child, I immediately connected with her. Even though the woman and I only spoke for a brief time, I thought about her and prayed for her constantly.

I didn't need to call a volunteer coordinator or show up at a scheduled time to serve. I served a stranger I would most likely never see again with prayer. Even bigger than this, I saw serving others in new ways—ways involving more than my standard ideas about serving with money and time. Serving others started to mean actively loving those around me.

In the Christian classic, *Practicing the Presence of God*, Brother Lawrence sums it up when he says, "Never tire of doing even the smallest things for Him, because He isn't impressed so much with the dimensions of our work as with the love in which it was done."[4]

Simply put, our family started to notice people and then, act out of love.

"A new command I give you: Love one another. As I have loved you, so you must love one another. By this, everyone will know you are my disciples, if you love one another" (John 13:34-35).

Let's Get Practical

After each chapter, the *Let's Get Practical* section gives quick take-away strategies relating to the chapter and easy ideas you can implement in your home, your community, and the world. Since this chapter focused on just starting, let's go ahead and just start.

In Your Home

- **Pray.** Flip to the *31 Days of Growing a Giving Heart* prayer calendar in the back of the book. Tear out the page and hang it on your refrigerator. Carve out time each day to look up and pray over the listed verse.

In Your Community

- **Research organizations.** What established nonprofit or charity organizations are up and moving?

- **Surround yourself with people who inspire.** Engage in conversations with those you know who are already up to good.
- **Join a book club.** Look for a local book club, and when it's your turn to choose, pick a book that gets others-centered conversation started. (See ***Books that Inspire Action*** for ideas.)

In the World

- **Take to social media.** Follow organizations online that get your heart pumping. Keep updated on happenings.
- **Don't forget the blogs.** People around the world share every kind of experience online in stories and pictures. Engage in online conversation.

Dinner Table Dialogue

Dinnertime is the perfect time to chat it up. Consider and discuss the following questions:

- What does your family hope to accomplish by serving others? Do you want to get to know your community? Build relationships? Offer support to the hurting?
- What would you like service to look like in your family?
- What time frame are you considering?

CHAPTER 4

GENEROUS WITH YOUR SKILLS
Why Lip Synching Isn't a Talent

━━

I used to think the words "Fantasy Football" and "ministry" never went together. Now, I'm about 60-percent certain they can.

In sixth grade, my friends and I signed up for a school-wide talent show. I secretly dreamed of standing on-stage and reciting poetry. However, being socially aware, I knew reciting poetry on-stage translated into eternal dorkdom, and I decided to showcase my skills in a hipper way: lip syncing Madonna's "Like a Virgin."

Sixth grade, people.

My lip-syncing dance crew realized a four-star performance takes planning and preparation, and we threw ourselves into both. Preparation included figuring out answers to the following important questions:

- What would we wear?
- What color puffy paint should accent our shoes?
- Should we leave our hair down or pull it back?
- Could we possibly sneak "stage makeup" from our mothers?
- And again, what would we wear?

Although our group met frequently, we never practiced our dance routine. We all knew the song, so mouthing the words came easily. And the dance steps? Oh, those little details always fall together. Right?

The dance routine never fell together, and on the day of the talent show, our five-person crew stood on a dark stage in a stinky gym. A red jam box blared something about "being touched for the very first time." We mouthed words into our fake microphones, and danced the one move we knew: step, sway, step, sway, step, sway. Pretending to dance for three minutes on a dark stage taught me two things:

- No one pays attention to matching puffy-painted shoes in a dark, stinky gym.
- God gives us talents, all of us, but ignoring your talent (poetry), and going for a cooler talent (lip syncing) doesn't work.

The tough part about being generous with your talents is not the being generous part. Acknowledging God gives us talents proves a much harder concept to believe. I know what you are thinking. It's the same thing everyone thinks when they ponder the skills they possess.

Talents? What talents?

God made billowy clouds, glowing bugs, flowering cacti, and our complex, trillion-celled bodies. When we see these magnificent mysteries, we believe that's God, but we struggle with buying into the idea that God created us with special care and planned each of our gifts and abilities. Even before we entered the world, God knew us (Jeremiah 1:5).

We dismiss our uniqueness, and most of us maintain an all-or-nothing attitude. If I'm not really good at _____ (fill in the blank), I must stink.

The idea that your skills mean little is completely false, but this belief keeps us stagnant.

Consider your life experiences. No one lives the life you live. Your story, the one that started long before you remember, is unlike anyone else's story. Every victory you celebrate and every trial you endure mold you into the perfect person for the plans God holds for you.

Don't believe me? Take a quick peek at a few details from my life.

- My mother gave birth to me, her first-born, at age nineteen.
- My parents divorced when I was in second grade.
- When I enrolled in ninth grade, I found myself at my tenth school.
- I graduated from college, the first in my family.
- Our oldest daughter needed supplemental oxygen for her first three-and-one-half years of life.

There you have it. Five random facts from my life. Some interesting, but for the most part, all pretty average. However, if I look closer, I see how each of these events shaped me. The stories of teenage moms cry out to me. I understand long-term effects of divorce. I seek out friends and easily establish communities. I value education. My heart aches for parents of chronically ill children.

I look at my thirty-eight years and see history and hurts, but God sees His creation living the life He planned, *to each according to each one's unique ability* (Matthew 25:15). Through my life experiences, I developed a set of unique skills—a set of skills different from yours, but a special set of abilities God expects me to use.

Um, My Skills May Be Lost. How Do I Find Them?

Just as I listed facts from my life, create a list of details and events about yours. You may not think growing up on a ranch in Montana stands out, but it does. You may wonder what being an only child has to do with anything, but trust me, it's unique. You may find the fact that you speak two languages common, but it's not.

Once you develop a list, stop and evaluate its content. Think about the impact these details have had on you and the skills that developed as a result of these experiences. Then, consider trying the following:

Discovering Your Skills Strategy #1: Ask yourself what you enjoy.

Look in the mirror. You possess ease in handling conflict. You excel in the kitchen. Some stare at a pile of junk mail and see a mess; you stare at the pile and an organization system forms in your head. Maybe you paint walls, or maybe you paint canvas. Others may look at a baseball team of ten-year-olds and see a headache; you look at them and see raw talent. The areas you enjoy are often areas in which you excel.

In Brad Meltzer's book, *Heroes For My Son*, Meltzer discusses his friends Joe Shuster and Jerry Siegel. Shuster and Siegel grew up during the Great Depression, loved drawing, and dreamed of creating a superhero.

A hand-drawn superhero during the Depression? Can you hear the disapproving comments?

"Give it up!"

"Get a job!"

"Grow up!"

However, Shuster and Siegel refused to relinquish their dream. They enjoyed drawing, and these boys possessed both skills and determination. Too poor to buy drawing materials, they drew on butcher paper. When people deemed their idea foolish, they improved their work and pitched it again. In the end, Shuster and Siegel took something they enjoyed and turned it into more than a dream attained. For a country in desperate need of something to believe in, Shuster and Siegel used Superman as a symbol of hope.[1]

Discovering Your Skills Strategy #2: Listen when others compliment you.

Sometimes you receive sincere compliments. For me, this is difficult. I cringe at the extra attention, deflect quickly, and move on to the next subject as soon as possible. Is your reaction to compliments similar to mine? If so, the next time someone pays you a compliment, resist the urge to dismiss praise. Stop and pay attention.

When someone states you do something well, or you should do more of another thing, listen to what is being said. Others notice skills we miss. Our talents may be difficult for us to acknowledge, but the skills of others are easy to see.

Often gifts pop from people's personalities.

If I introduced you to my friend, Susan, she would be thrilled to meet you. Susan would greet you with hugs and then begin to dig and unearth details about your life. With only one question, Susan brings up stories from long ago that you thought were lost. Soon, you think Susan looks very familiar. Maybe it's because of her sweet face, but most likely it's because she feels like an old friend.

Susan's ability to make people feel special and at ease is a skill—a skill that others quickly notice.

Discovering Your Skills Strategy #3: Reflect on activities you loved as a child.

What did you spend your time doing when pay, recognition, and adult obligations didn't matter? I played teacher with neighbor kids. I planned events and parties with friends. I wrote a mini-newspaper. I spent most of my free moments outdoors. While growing up, I spent my time enjoying the above activities. And guess what? I happen to have skills in each of the above.

My friend's husband, Trey, is a typical type-A engineer who loves football. Trey views part of his ministry as organizing a fantasy football league. At first, I thought, *Trey uses that excuse so he can spend hours upon hours being the commissioner of a pretend football league while his wife completes every chore imaginable around the house.*

But then, a few years went by, and instead of the fantasy football league remaining an event guys participated in behind isolated computer screens, the men involved met in person. They developed real relationships, and the league even brought guys with zero interest in all things God into contact with guys who loved the Lord in big ways.

Trey combined his leadership and organizational skills with something he was passionate about: football. Despite my shock and disbelief, fantasy football proved valuable. But don't worry. I won't tell your husbands this annoying fact.

Now you have a list of unique facts about yourself. You know what you enjoy and what others think you excel in. You've spent a little time pondering the longings of your childhood heart, and hopefully you've come to the conclusion that you possess skills and abilities.

What Does God Say about Using Our Talents?

Long ago, talent meant a unit of weight. Later, a talent constituted a group of coins worth more than a thousand dollars. Today, we know talent means ability. Matthew 25:14-30 tells the story of growing talents—the cold, hard, moolah kind of talents.

> *Again, it will be like a man going on a journey, who called his servants and entrusted his property to them. To one he gave five talents of money, to another two talents, and to another one talent, each according to his ability. Then he went on his journey. The man who received the five talents went at once and put his money to work and gained five more. So also, the one with the two talents gained two more. But the man who had received the one talent went off, dug a hole in the ground and hid his master's money.*

Dig, dig, dig.

Plop.

Cover, cover, cover.

Of course, when the master returned, he celebrated the two servants who used their talents to create more wealth for him. What smart servants! Then, the master condemned the servant who foolishly buried the gift he received and shoved that worthless servant out the door and into the darkness.

Why would a person take such a gift—in this case, a whole load of money—and bury it? Fear? Yes. Insecurity? Yes. Laziness? Yes.

Now let's talk about our talents. Not the moolah kind of talents, but the ability kind of talents. The gifts that make you … well, you. How many times do we respond like the shovel-carrying third servant? We fear. Therefore, we do nothing. We worry what others will think, and we do nothing. We find ourselves torn between "I must do everything" and "I can't do anything." These thoughts paralyze us, and—you guessed it— we do nothing. Maybe we don't throw our talents in the ground and toss a bunch of dirt on them, but we ignore them.

Ways to Keep Your Talents Locked Away and Never Use Them for Others

Converse with real or imaginary critics.

Often, the urge to use our talents or skills is strong, but the fear of our skills being rejected is stronger. When I started writing, I frequently imagined what I'd say to those who questioned my writing skills.

Oh, writing? Yes, it's a hobby I don't put much time into. Lie. I dismissed my ability before anyone else could.

Oh, that article? I threw it on paper in an hour. I can't believe they published it. Big lie. I worked an hour-and-a-half on the query letter alone.

I even conjured up reasons I continued to write. *It's a creative outlet to keep me from becoming lost in mommyhood.* Big fat lie. I loved to write before I could spell.

Then came the day when my imaginary conversations with critics turned real. Someone close to me questioned the time I put in and the results I received from my writing. Translation: Amy sucks.

The words burned. My head spun, and my imagination suited up. I played out situations in which I told her off. I envisioned myself reciting all the ways I supported her. I conceived the content of an imaginary letter. Then, one day, I realized that replaying a hypothesized conversation gobbled up loads of time in my head. Time I wanted to spend creating. I learned that allowing criticism to fester blocked creativity.

Today, I work hard to ignore my real critics and close the door on imaginary ones, as well.

Entertain the ugly "j" word.

Normally, jealousy leaves me alone. However, sometimes when things fall into place for her or him or her, I find myself comparing my abilities to someone else's. And when I compare myself to others, I always fall short. I wonder why rainbows appear when they work hard, but when I work hard it keeps raining. The talents of others surround me, and if I'm honest, sometimes the talents of others make me question the value of my own talents.

I have a friend who is *that mom*. The mom who allows her kids to write with chalk on the walls and bakes cakes that look like magical dreamlands and choreographs dance routines with her kids just for fun. So when *that mom* offhandedly asked if I knew of a good papier-mâché mix because she hoped to create her own Easter baskets, I let the j-word creep in. Am I less because my kids' Easter baskets come from the dollar bin? Am I less because I'm not mixing messes in my kitchen? I start to doubt my parenting abilities because someone else happens to be a super fun mom.

I watch my photographer friend snap a random shot of a dead flower, and its beauty reminds me of life and I want to hang it on my wall. I see my husband learn a lawn game in minutes, and within hours he could be an Olympic cornhole champion.

Here's the kicker: If I stop and think about my jealous thoughts and the reasons surrounding them, I become embarrassed. Embarrassed because I don't want to master papier-mâché or be a champion cornhole player, and I realize I'm jealous of abilities I don't even want. Comparing my abilities to those of others keeps me from embracing the skills I have.

Debate your impact.

Why bother using your talents if they don't translate into success? I think anyone who considers using their skills debates their intended impact. Often, if we push through, battle our inner critics, and use our abilities, we become hung up on measurable impact. When we commit to join an organization, travel with a club, teach a class, or mentor a child, we expect our efforts to influence someone in a positive way. It makes sense. If I put myself out there, I want to make a difference. While this way of thinking seems logical, it holds us back.

When we get hung up on our impact, we stand in a slippery place. Why? Because it isn't about *our* impact. It's about His. If we constantly calculate and measure the worthiness of what we are doing, talents and skills become about us. We start looking for results other than His glory. Sometimes we look for applause. Sure, maybe it isn't the standing-on-stage kind of applause, but we search out affirmation, and we seek acknowledgement. Even in our desire to use our skills in a way to help others, we place ourselves at the center of our thoughts.

In 2009, Jade Sims decided crafters could, and should, rally together for good. With this goal in mind, Jade asked friends to create pillowcase dresses for girls residing in Mexican orphanages.

> "I received twenty-nine pillowcase dresses, and I was over the moon."

Twenty-nine dresses. While some may have become frustrated—what's twenty-nine dresses to hundreds of orphans?—Jade celebrated. Twenty-nine pillowcase dresses meant twenty-nine girls would feel the love of strangers.

> "At the time, I had no idea what was coming. The next project is when it really hit me that we could make a difference. A blogging friend contacted me and wanted us to make dolls for orphans in Nicaragua through the Orphan Network. We received over 400 handmade dolls. My mind was blown, and I realized we were on to something good."

Something good, indeed. Today, Craft Hope—an online community of crafters founded by Jade—has distributed over 100 thousand handmade goods to people all over the world. Despite Craft Hope's success, Jade understands each handmade item is special, and Jade still celebrates the small.

> "Some of my favorite donations have been from an individual and come as one item in one box. The idea that one person learned to sew and made a doll or blanket for a stranger brings me to tears."[2]

Jade did not get hung up on her impact, and her impact exploded. Jade's story reminds me we aren't the evaluators or directors of our influence.

Isn't measuring our impact made easier when we acknowledge the only One who evaluates us is God? God refuses to judge how many people you helped when you volunteered your accounting skills during tax season. God overlooks the fact that those cars you washed to raise money could have been cleaner. God dismisses the fact that the cookies you baked for the new neighbor are premade. He just wants you to turn on the oven. He doesn't even care if you end up scraping off the burnt part on the bottom of the cookie.

Go Ahead. Start.

When our family first looked for ways to become involved in our community, I dismissed opportunities because I deemed us unqualified.

- We don't know how to knit!
- My kids can't clean well.
- What do we know about gardening?
- I think that's pretty far to walk if we're just picking up garbage.

I found our skills subpar in every area, including garbage pickup. Then, we received a call. Would our family be willing to work the kids' arts and craft section at a small community festival?

I grilled the caller. Will I have to paint? Because I don't paint. And will I have to draw? Because I don't draw. And will I have to mix colors? Because I think yellow and red make orange, but I'm not positive. And does the caller happen to know what people mean by primary colors? Because I seem to have forgotten.

Finally, after much reassurance that zero art skills were required to volunteer in the arts and crafts area, and I learned our family would only be responsible for cleaning paint brushes and wiping off tables, I signed up.

The day of the festival arrived. We walked ourselves to the arts and crafts table and discovered that one of the face painters hadn't shown up. Therefore, the Sullivans would be painting faces, and could we please hurry because the line was already ten kids deep?

I tried to explain our lack of art skills, but no one seemed to listen. Instead, a chatty little boy kept interrupting me and saying he wanted to be a puma.

I grabbed a brush, and I painted him into a cat. He didn't seem to notice pumas don't have triangle noses. The next little girl asked for a butterfly, and I painted two polka dot blobs with antenna. Huh, she liked it. Then, before I knew it, I was cranking out really bad cartoon pictures. And guess what? No one complained about my face-painting skills.

At this point, I fully expected my family to abandon me and hide out by the food in the corner of the festival, but when I looked up, I saw my husband adding some crazy-looking fish to a huge river banner as my daughter sat next to him painting swirly objects.

No one asked me about primary colors or mixing paint, and our short time under that pavilion at the arts and crafts booth taught me that serving isn't always about skills. Sometimes, it's just about being willing to show up and stretch yourself a little.

Let's Get Practical

There's no denying you've got skills. Go use them. Become generous with your skills and talents in the following ways:

In Your Home

- **Be an example to your kids and use your talents.** You know how to tend a garden (Well, actually, I don't, but you might!). Take the time and show a friend how to grow a mean tomato plant.
- **Go on an electronics fast.** See what activities you enjoy when you aren't plugged in.
- **Plan creativity.** Give your child resources and encourage him or her to use those sticks lying around the yard, the crayons collecting dust, or the mismatched socks your washer produces.

In Your Community

- **Think about specific trials you endured.** Have skills or insight come from these events? Would you be willing to share your experiences?
- **Jump online and investigate ways you can help.** No commitments. You aren't signing up for anything. See what is available in your community. Here's a fabulous national website to help you with this task: HandsOn Network (http://www.handsonnetwork.org).
- **Expose your child to a variety of people and activities.** Give your kids permission to experience new things. Visit a dairy farm or downtown Dallas or Des Moines or Denmark. Just go, and then learn from the places you go.
- **Share your child's artwork.** Let your children see there is value in the work they create.

In The World

- **Invite an international missionary to your church, women's luncheon, or small group.** Let the guest of honor describe different types of skills that would help them. Opportunities are endless: prayer partner, social media assistant, ghostwriter to assist in the upkeep of a website.

- **Memorize the following verse:** *Each one should use whatever gift he has received to serve others, faithfully administering God's grace in its various forms* (1 Peter 4:10).
- **Check out VolunteerMatch.org** to find virtual volunteer opportunities from all over the world based on your area of interest. Current opportunities include graphic designer, teddy bear knitter, copy editor, grant writer, illustrator of cartoons, and over 4,000 additional listings for volunteers.

Dinner Table Dialogue

- Talk about the activities you loved as a child. Tell your kids about the clubs and sports you participated in when you were their age.
- Ask your child about his or her favorite way to spend free time.
- Discuss the gifts and talents you see in each other.
- What is a skill you wish you possessed? Why?
- Can you think of a way to use your talents to help others?

CHAPTER 5
GENEROUS WITH STRANGERS
Roadside Births

I used to think of strangers as a danger. You know—stranger danger. Now, I think of strangers as people who can help you when you are giving birth on the side of the road.

I gave birth to our second-born on the side of the road. I'm certain God concluded this event would be a fantastic way to teach me about the kindness of strangers.

Strangers. Yuck. Even the word sounds creepy and conjures up a boatload of negative images: weird men lurking, dishonest thieves stealing, perverted molesters luring, a strange guy climbing into your home through an open window and kidnapping your only daughter.

Whew, I lost myself. But those situations happen. Just watch the news. Evil-doers walk our streets, and we must beware. You know this attitude, because this is what we are spoon-fed from childhood.

As a child, I remember my mom reading me the book *Never Talk to Strangers* by Irma Joyce. In the oversized, purple book, cartoon animals approach smiling children, and readers are reminded again and again never to talk to strangers.

Yes. Children shouldn't talk to strangers, because they haven't developed the discernment to recognize potentially dangerous situations. However, throughout the years, "beware of strangers" grew from a cautionary warning to a mantra believed by the masses.

Back to the roadside birth.

God wanted me to stop and notice strangers and heroes placed in my own life, but I refused. *Sorry, God, I'm much too busy for people I don't know.* God didn't like my answer, so He made a stranger notice me.

Pregnant with my second child, I resolved to teach until my due date. My motto? "Unless you see this (rocking my arms as if holding a baby), you will see me here." I didn't want to work until the very last day of my pregnancy because of my stellar work ethic. Nope, I simply didn't have enough days saved for time off. I wanted every possible second with my new baby, and it didn't matter how uncomfortable I was. My pregnant self remained at work.

A quick summary and timeline of the events leading up to the birth of Baby #2:

1:35 pm	Hmmm, that hurt. I wonder if it's a contraction.
1:45 pm	Yep, woo, strong contractions. I should leave.
1:47 pm	Get my keys and coat and start for the door. Co-workers intervene. "You can't drive yourself!"
1:50 pm	Call mildly annoyed husband. "Are you sure this is it?" he prods (hoping not, since he's in the middle of a basketball game he's winning).
2:10 pm	I can't take the pain!
2:15 pm	Friend insists we drive to meet mildly annoyed husband. The school nurse jumps in the car "just in case."
2:17 pm	My water breaks in friend's car.
2:17-2:35 pm	Stuck in construction traffic.
2:36 pm	Meet husband and take the school nurse with us "just in case." See a police car. Can he escort us?
2:37 pm	Pass police escort who is puttering along. Call an ambulance to meet us at an upcoming exit.

2:39 pm	Arrive at exit, pull over, and wait for an ambulance. Policeman catches up with us, and another cop car stops. A fire engine stops. I'm not sure what a fire engine does during labor, but WHERE IS THAT *%$# AMBULANCE?

I am not someone who desires to partake in a natural delivery. No way, friends. Not this girl. I want the hot tub, soft music, dim lighting, and a big fat epidural—none of which seemed to be happening. At this point, I used strong language again to let everyone know my feelings about the situation.

I may have scared the police. I know I scared my husband. Everyone else continued to stare off into the distance, trying to collectively will the ambulance to us. The school nurse looked concerned, and I wondered if we had arrived at "just in case."

Did I mention my pants were now off?

I was sitting in our jeep on the side of the road, emergency service people surrounded me, and I was pant-less. Nice.

A woman I don't know, a total stranger, drove by this crazy scene and stopped.

I can't tell you how many accidents and stalled cars I've passed in my life. Why would I stop? I'm sure someone has things under control, and that someone is not me. I have to be at _____ (fill in the blank). I'm late. I'm busy. I wouldn't know what to do even if I did stop. Someone else will step in to fix that flat tire, call for help, or offer assistance. Again, that someone is not me. It has never been me. But thankfully, that someone was Denna Reese.

Denna and my school nurse talked quietly, and the ambulance arrived.

For some reason, I thought everything would be solved once the ambulance arrived. As unrealistic as it sounds, I thought the emergency medical service guys might jump out of the vehicle and give me a big shot of something . . . preferably morphine. However, the reality of the situation was one EMT had never delivered a baby and the other had—eight years ago!—and, sadly, the ambulance didn't contain an epidural.

2:48 pm	I'm crammed into the ambulance, and Denna offers to go with. See, Denna is a nurse.
2:54 pm	Denna tells the ambulance to pull over despite my screaming for a hospital bed. Denna tells me if I push once, it will be over.
2:58 pm	Ruby Catherine Sullivan is born on I-26 on the side of the road at Exit 18.

Later, when I asked Denna about the birth of my daughter, she replied, "I thought someone needed help."

Nowadays, Denna is no longer a stranger. In fact, she was one of the few guests at a certain girl's first birthday celebration.

How selfless. How unlike me. But oh, how I'd like to be. How God desires for all of us to be.

Yes, God, I get it. My lesson in strangers. All strangers aren't bad. In fact, some strangers can be heroes. Denna Reese arrived in my life so I could get a tiny glimpse of You.

The Strangers Who Surround You

In the book, *Praying for Strangers*, River Jordan discusses her ambitious New Year's resolution. In 2009, Jordan decides to pray for a complete stranger every day for an entire year.

Jordan takes readers with her as she encounters a variety of people: a bruised teen, angry mother, homeless man, hotel maid, young farmhand, and a cast of other unique individuals. Daily, Jordan learns names, hears stories, and prays for people she doesn't know.

As I read about the strangers Jordan meets, I lounge in a chair at a mega bookstore. My chair is one of five cushy chairs lined up in front of three oversized tables. Facing me is another row of five identical cushy chairs. Each chair contains a person. Basically, I am situated among nine other people, and without looking up, I am certain of one thing: I have no idea what *any* of the people who surround me look like.

I try to quiz myself. Surely I can remember a face or some small detail about the strangers who surround me. I have spent over an hour in the same chair, but sadly, I recall nothing.

I look up, and the fog lifts. The once-blurry bodies take on faces and expressions.

One chair over from me sits a young woman. Her hands tightly grip the book she is reading, and entwined in her fingers, she holds a crumpled tissue. Her posture is rigid, her eyes watery.

I pretend to grab something out of my purse so I can peek at her book. It's about divorce. Minutes later, two kids wander up to her. They want to go home. The woman nods, lays the book on the coffee table, and leaves.

For the rest of the day, I think of the woman. What's her story? Does she have the support of friends and family? How will she make it on her own? How are her children?

I also wonder about all the people I neglect to notice—the people who interact with me at work, stand next to me in line, or pass me on the street. Do I make time to see beyond my busyness and glimpse into their lives?

Yep, It's Intimidating

My friend, Melody, once had a conversation with a Christian woman about the needy people in their area. Each year, this woman and her family anonymously adopt another family and leave bags of food and gifts on the family's front steps.

Melody writes:

> The families this woman donates to are families that are referred through the Department of Family and Children Services. Sometimes these "needy families" can be quite scary and intimidating.

> The more we talked, the more I heard her fears of these "type" of people rubbing off on her family. There was a strong desire for a healthy distance to be maintained. In all the years of giving, they never made face-to-face contact with the recipients of the gifts.

> I almost pictured "drive-by donations" taking place, where her family opened the sliding van door while still moving, thrust the bag of goods onto the porch, and then screeched

away on two wheels while saying a quick prayer. Who knows, maybe they even wore black stocking masks.

I love this Christian woman who does drive-by donations because she encourages her family to think of someone other than themselves. I also know there is a place for anonymous giving.

But I wonder how it might make a difference if this lady and her family walked up to the apartment doorstep and introduced themselves. Not for recognition but so a "next step" could be made. Maybe the next step is giving a bag of clothes and talking for a while and getting to know a tiny bit of the heart behind the name on the "needy list."

And what if, over time, the receiving family actually sat at this woman's dinner table one night? Imagine what God might do through an invitation like that.

Imagine, people. Imagine.

Looking for the Good, the Very, Very Good

When I hear stories from the Bible over and over, they lose the impact they had when I first heard them. I hate to admit it, but common verses and widely-known stories even seem a little b-o-r-i-n-g. However, when we dig and learn more about the context of the story and the time period in which it is being told, even familiar stories take on new meaning. Take a peek at this one.

One of the most-referenced examples of kindness towards strangers in the Bible is the story of the Good Samaritan (Luke 10:30-35). Yes, most of us know the story, but do you know that in Jesus' time, Jewish people certainly didn't think there was anything "good" about Samaritans?

Matt Williams describes it best in the *Becoming a Good Samaritan* DVD by saying, "To most Jewish people in Jesus' day, saying good Samaritan was like saying good Al-Qaeda terrorist. A good terrorist? Most would argue, is there such a thing?"[1]

Williams continues to explain that Samaritans and Jews had quite a history. You see, about 150 years before Jesus lived, the Jews destroyed a Samaritan temple. Then, a few years before Jesus, the Samaritans defiled a Jewish temple by scattering human bones all over. Yuck, right? Surely not a sign of anything good.

In fact, the Jewish people and Samaritans disliked each other so much that during this time some Jews prayed that the Samaritans, also referred to as "the stupid people," would not receive eternal life from God. Yikes. Praying against eternal life?

Again, not good. Very not good.

As we delve into this story, we learn that a Jewish man walked the very dangerous 17-mile stretch between Jerusalem and New Jericho. Peter Lawrence Alexander describes this stretch of land:

> Some say it was called the Ascent of Blood because of the red rock in the limestone on the mountainside. I like that explanation. But others say it was called the Ascent of Blood because of the number of people attacked by thieves and robbers.[2]

This Jewish man was beaten, robbed, and left to die on the side of this narrow, winding road.

The first person to come across this hurt and naked man was a priest. Williams details the many reasons most travelers would refuse to offer help. First, the priest couldn't tell by this man's clothes (because he wasn't wearing much!) what religion this man was. Many texts instructed Jewish people not to help sinners. If this man happened to be a Gentile and the priest touched him, the priest would become unclean. In addition, if this poor, naked man was actually dead and the priest touched him, it would be even worse. The priest would become ceremonially unclean, rendering him unable to perform his priestly duties. It made perfect sense for the priest to walk by this man, because helping a sinner could actually be seen as a sin. Bottom line: The priest had the legal right to keep walking, and keep walking is exactly what he did.[3]

Again, not good.

Next came the Levite, who probably knew the priest traveled ahead of him on the road. The Levite reasoned that if the priest didn't stop to help this man, he should just keep walking as well, which is exactly what he did. The priest led by example, and the Levite followed. Not good.

The next person traveling the road was a Samaritan, one of the "stupid people." If the Samaritan stopped, he too could face consequences. The Samaritan rode a donkey, and by taking the time to stop, the Samaritan put himself in danger of being robbed. However, the Samaritan didn't worry about losing his donkey. He was more concerned about the beaten man. Without thinking of himself or the consequences he might face for helping this man, the Samaritan stopped. Determining the man needed more help than he could give, he put the man on his donkey and took him to an inn.

Another potential problem? It didn't look good for a Samaritan man to show up at a Jewish inn with a Jewish man, who was beaten so badly he couldn't talk. What if people thought it was the Samaritan who beat the man? An angry Jew might try to take revenge. However, the Samaritan didn't worry about that either. He was more concerned about the beaten man.[4]

The Samaritan could have dropped the man off with someone and continued on his way, but he didn't. Instead, he paid the innkeeper to take care of this man and asked him to let him know if he needed more money. The Samaritan didn't worry about the history of the Samaritans and the Jews. He wasn't angry about destroyed temples. He wasn't thinking, "I'm late, I'm late, I'm late." He saw a hurting person. He saw an opportunity to help.

And what he did for a total stranger was very, very good.

Let's Get Practical

What does this mean to us? Allowing your children to interact with strangers can be scary. Start on a level that makes you comfortable.

In Your Home

- **Become a pen pal.** Today, miles separate many families, and oftentimes, children don't have a close relationship with their relatives. Choose an aunt, cousin, or other distant family member and commit to writing this person regularly.
- **Invite someone outside of your family to participate in a family event or holiday.** You may think the person will feel weird about this, but trust me, they won't. This is coming from the girl who cried all of Christmas 2003 because our family of three spent it alone.
- **Research your family history.** Many of our relatives' stories are unknown, and people even a few generations back are strangers to us. How far can you trace your family's ancestry? Recently, we looked up the Sullivan family crest. We learned more about the history of our last name, and it pushed us to dig and learn about the people who came before us.

In Your Community

- **Encourage each person in your family to pray for one stranger each day for a week.** Share about the people you've encountered.
- **Hold a block party.** (Or, for you country folks who don't live in neighborhoods, forget the word "block" and just host a party and invite people you want to know better.) Do not even think about making it fancy. Have everyone bring a dish. Focus on friends and not frills.
- **Attend community events.** Yes, church events prove fun, but you know those people already. Seek out new faces by attending events planned in your community.

In The World

- **Tour a local service agency that serves a national or international population with your family.** Although interaction with the agency's clients may not always be feasible or appropriate, the agency's staff may offer ideas for indirect involvement. For example, the staff at a local shelter, which serves battered women and children, encourages families to bake cookies for those who reside there. Although volunteers don't always get to see or meet people who reside at the shelter, they do get a peek into the lives of families who use the facility.
- **Pay attention to national and international news.** Pick out leaders, politicians, and people mentioned within the articles, and pray for them.
- **Look for already-established drives serving the international community.** Each year, organizations run all kinds of drives; agencies collect food, coats, shoes, school supplies, personal hygiene products, and loads of other items. Watch for ways your family can participate, and then, pray for the agencies hosting the drive and the people who receive the donations.

Dinner Table Dialogue

- How do you welcome people you don't know into your life?
- How do you interact with people you don't know?
- Name a person you'd like to know better.
- How can you encourage relationships to grow beyond the surface level?
- What opportunities are you missing out on because you overlook the strangers in your life?

CHAPTER 6

GENEROUS WITH FORGIVENESS
Holding Grudges is Selfish

I used to think forgiving transgressions made you weak. Then, people reminded me Jesus was certainly not weak.

All of us experience hurt on both small and catastrophic levels. A dissolving friendship, an abusive parent, slanderous gossip, an unfaithful spouse, addiction to porn, aversion to food, an act against our children, incest, murder, deceit, and sadly, a list of wrongs can never include all of the devastating trials we face.

Often, we walk through painful experiences, plodding through hurt and plowing through days while a sense of heaviness lingers and resentment builds. While forgiveness seems good in theory, it proves difficult for me to practice.

I struggle to forgive. Not because I want to be mean or hold onto wrongs, but because of my tendency to be a smidge selfish. I think about my rights, hurts, and pride, and after much evaluation, my injury often trumps your forgiveness.

In middle school, I knew a girl named Erin. She owned all things important: enough Swatches to line her forearm, all shirts Esprit, all jeans Guess, the coveted Keds, a seat at the cool table, and a gaggle of followers ready to laugh at all things Erin deemed funny.

And Erin thought I was funny—the wrong kind of funny. A year filled with whispers, laughter directed toward me, continuous eye rolling, and snide remarks left me broken. Quickly, that brokenness turned to anger, which turned to hatred. When I saw Erin, I seethed.

However, I didn't have to see Erin for long, because a year after I met her, I moved. But when I moved, I took Erin with me—in my head. She lurked in my thoughts, and when I felt unsure of my appearance, she confirmed my insecurity.

Years later, I still evaluated my physical appearance through her middle-school eyes, and I still hated her. Then, one year during college, I returned home for Christmas break and saw Erin in a store. I stood and stared at the girl, now a woman, who I gave so much power to for over ten years.

Erin slid hanger after hanger aside until she noticed my stares. She looked up, held eye contact with me for a moment, smiled, and then continued sliding hangers. She had no idea who I was, and I no longer felt hatred toward her. I felt robbed of all the time I spent hating someone who couldn't even remember my name.

Forgiveness is a tricky little guy who hides in the corners of my heart and the dark places in my head, and I confess that skipping a chapter about being generous with forgiveness proved incredibly tempting.

What can *I* say about being generous with forgiveness?

I hold grudges, and it works for me.

Not only do I hold grudges for myself, but I happily hold grudges for my kids (who often forget to keep track of wrongs), my husband (who sees the good in everyone), and my friends (who deserve my loyalty). However, grudges can get heavy to lug around, especially if you carry the weight of grudges that aren't even your own. It is that weight that started my evaluation of forgiveness in my life.

Here's a snapshot of forgiveness in my life: You hurt me. We discuss it. I pretend to forgive you, or sometimes I don't pretend to forgive you. Then, I suggest we "move forward." That's a nice way of saying, "I'm not getting over how you wronged me for a long, long time, but I plan on pretending the wrong doesn't bother me just so I look good and you feel better."

My ideas on forgiveness always return to this: If I truly forgive you, I feel as if I condone your behavior. In addition, I see forgiveness as a sign of weakness. I think strong people are supposed to stand up for themselves and not allow others to walk all over them, and I perceive forgiveness as an invitation to be hurt again.

I like the sin of bitterness for a variety of reasons, but I especially like it because it can go virtually undetected. See, you can wrong me, and I can "forgive you," and things can look normal and shiny, but I've already built a partial wall blocking you out.

Unhealthy, I know, and that is probably why, in addition to having me write a book on serving when I'm clearly not the generous type, God also asked me to write a chapter on being generous with forgiveness when I'm not the forgiving type. To accomplish both a serving attitude and a forgiving spirit, God knew I needed to do more than just write about it. He knew I'd have to find a way to change.

I listen to my children, who are six years apart, as they play. I listen to them start "the fight." The one that's been around since the beginning of time. The fight known as "don't touch my stuff." The little one disrupted the order of the older one's belongings yet again. I remember having the exact argument with my sister years ago. My sister destroyed my pretend brick grocery store—complete with plastic food—daily. Now, my youngest daughter manhandles each delicate possession hidden in the corner of her older sister's dresser—possessions that are clearly in the "off limits" corner.

The girls bicker, and I linger in the other room, pretending not to notice the raised voices. I hear three words.

"I'm sorry, Iya."

And then I hear more.

"It's okay, Ruby. I forgive you."

Then, they go on. Just like that. They forget about the mess and hurt feelings, and they are off to something else.

Now, I don't say this to brag about my children's sweet sibling relationship, because I could write pages full of times when my girls' interactions didn't end so sweetly. I share this because I am amazed at how kids comprehend forgiveness.

The pessimistic part of me thinks kids understand forgiveness because they haven't lived enough to feel the emotions that come with being hurt repeatedly or being hurt in more serious ways. But, another part of me thinks kids understand unconditional love in a way adults struggle to comprehend.

In the eyes of children, petty wrongs often equal little more than wasted time, and the hurts of yesterday rarely carry over into the precious minutes of today. I want that attitude. I want to wake up each morning and truly give myself and those in my world a new start.

I recognize that holding on to bitterness hurts only me. I understand that forgiving others is an expectation God has for me. *For if you forgive men when they sin against you, your heavenly Father will also forgive you. But if don't forgive men their sins, your Father will not forgive your sins* (Matthew 6:14-15).

I need to know how forgiveness really works, and I need examples, but I also want you to know something important. The journey to forgiveness is something no person, book, or counselor can expect from you, and it is not my intention to tell you how to handle your hurt. It is only my intention to explore why I don't like to handle my own.

Therefore, because I'm a word person and because I learn best through stories, I seek out accounts of those who discover a way to forgive even the most horrific betrayals. I ask God to reveal Truth to me through the lives of people I know and through the lives of people I don't know, and in the end, through Jesus, who walked and talked and lived here on this crazy earth with us.

Forgiving a Killer

On October 2, 2006, Charles Roberts walked into the West Nickel Mines Amish School in Pennsylvania and ordered all the boys out of the building. Roberts then tied the hands and feet of ten young girls together. He stated he was "angry with God, and he needed to punish some Christian girls to get even with him."[1]

Then, Roberts shot ten girls, killing five of them before he killed himself.

The day after the shooting, a group of women visited the killer's widow to offer forgiveness. Later that week, the parents who had just buried their own daughters attended Roberts' funeral.[2] Soon after, the Amish community created a fund for the killer's widow and her three children.[3]

Both my mind and my heart struggle to comprehend forgiveness of this magnitude.

In the book *Amish Grace: How Forgiveness Transcended Tragedy*, authors Kraybill and Noldt describe forgiveness as a core part of the Amish culture.

After the 2006 schoolhouse shootings, Amish families fell back on a value ingrained in them: forgiveness. *Do not judge, and you will not be judged. Do not condemn, and you will not be condemned. Forgive, and you will be forgiven* (Luke 6:37).

Those outside of the small Amish community stood in shock and confusion. To the outside world, the idea of forgiveness at a time of such intense sorrow seemed incomprehensible. To the Amish, forgiveness was deeply rooted in their culture.

The authors explain it further.

> *We all embrace patterns of behavior and habits of the mind that shape what we do in a given situation. Culture is the term we use for a group's repertoire of beliefs and behaviors. It involves assumptions and conduct that are so deeply rooted and so often practiced that most people are not even aware of them. Culture reflects people's history and teaching, and is especially visible in times of stress that demand immediate response, where there is no time or emotional energy to think through all the possible actions.[4]*

By reaching out to the killer's family, the Amish simply practiced what they knew to be true. They didn't form committees regarding the steps they would take following the shooting. When faced with a stressful situation that required immediate response, they acted.

Later, in *Amish Grace*, Kraybill interviews an Amish man named Amos, who explains the ideas that motivated the Amish to act in more detail.

"When you start looking in the New Testament," Amos says, "it's the first thing that's there. That's what the Bible is all about: forgiveness. It says we are to take up our cross and follow Jesus. No matter what happens, we must follow him." Amos goes on to say, "Just look at Matthew, Mark, Luke, and John. They're all about forgiveness. You don't have to go far in the New Testament and you find it all over the place. Look at the Sermon on the Mount. It's filled with forgiveness."[5]

While the world watched an Amish community handle an unthinkable tragedy, we were reminded of the gift we received in exchange for forgiveness of our sin: God's gift of his only Son. *He who did not spare his own son, but gave him up for us all* (Romans 8:32a).

Forgiving an Abuser

As a preteen, Geoff was abused by a trusted adult. This abuse triggered shame, guilt, and a great deal of anger. For years, Geoff struggled with his past. Then, one day, Geoff found his abuser sitting close to him at a café.

> *I walked over to him. I introduced myself and told him what he had done to me as a child and how it had affected me. He was a big man, and he tried to stand up and protest. I put my hand out and told him to sit down. He obeyed immediately. I told him that despite what he had done I was going to forgive him. I told him twice. He looked totally broken. It was as if my forgiveness shattered him.[6]*

Powerful.

Liar, Liar

If there is one guy in the Bible who understands sin and the impact of forgiveness, it's David. Why David? Well, to understand forgiveness, you need to comprehend sin. And David is a man who knew both—well.

A handsome young shepherd, David was handpicked by the Lord (1 Samuel 16:12). From the beginning, David had things going for him. For starters, he noticed God everywhere, especially in nature while he tended sheep. Noticing God's creations led David to singing and writing passionate poems of praise. You know his work—those little ole things we call the Psalms. While David spilled out his feelings of awe and lifted up his love to God, God noticed and looked happily on David.

God protected David against his enemies. As a teenager, David defeated a nine-foot giant with a single rock to the forehead (1 Samuel 17:49). And later, when David's jealous father-in-law, Saul, tried to shoot David with arrows (1 Samuel 18:10-11), God protected David again. God's shelter of David didn't end there either.

Saul sent David into battle with thousands of troops in hopes that David would be killed in war (1 Samuel 18:13), but God guarded David. Saul even led an extensive manhunt to put David to death, but once again, God shielded David from harm (1 Samuel 19). Through the many dangers David encountered, God blessed him and always had David return to Israel as a celebrated hero who was loved by many. More favor.

Through all of the fighting and leading and hiding and fleeing, David survived. Not only did he survive. David became King of Israel.

And once this young shepherd became a privileged king and obtained power, what did he do with it? He seduced another man's wife, Bathsheba. And when Bathsheba became pregnant, David arranged for her husband to be placed on the frontlines of a battlefield and killed. Then, David lied, deceived, and even attempted to cover his tracks (2 Samuel 11). David brazenly abused the power God granted him.

Oh, and it gets worse.

We expect David to confess his sins. But no, David does not admit his wrongdoing. In fact, he refuses to acknowledge his misdeeds to even himself, and instead, David carries the heavy burden of shame and guilt with him.

David keeps his secret sins hidden, and we all know how it is to carry secret sin. Our sins may be different from David's, but we all have them: the endless spending, the crush on that certain married guy, the constant coveting, the infrequent social drinking that turns into something you need daily.

Initially, secret sin gives us a high, a type of rush. We feel untouchable in an I'm-on-top-of-the-world kind of way, but soon we become caught up in our secret sin. Eventually, a nagging feeling shows up. Then, our sin becomes hot and it proves heavy. Our thoughts become foggy, relationships suffer, and we find ourselves clinging to something our friends and family know little about.

Eventually, as David describes in Psalm 38:3, his sin even impacts him physically.

> *Because of your wrath there is no health in my body; my bones have no soundness because of my sin. My guilt has overwhelmed me like a burden too heavy to bear. My wounds fester and are loathsome because of my sinful folly. I am bowed down and brought very low; all day long I go about mourning. My back is filled with searing pain; there is no health in my body. I am feeble and utterly crushed; I groan in anguish of heart.*

Sounds terrible, right? But it doesn't end there. Psalm 38:10-11 continues on.

> *My heart pounds, my strength fails me; even the light has gone from my eyes. My friends and companions avoid me because of my wounds; my neighbors stay far away.*

Just when you think David could be crushed by the weight of his sins, God sends the prophet, Nathan, to confront David, and in 2 Samuel Chapter 12, Nathan lays David's sin out in front of him big time.

> *This is what the Lord, the God of Israel, says: I anointed you king over Israel, I delivered you from the hand of Saul. I gave your master's house to you, and your master's wives into your arms. I gave you the house of Israel and Judah. And if all this had been too little, I would have given you even more. Why did you despise the word of the Lord by doing what is evil in his eyes?*

Finally, David confesses.

Guess what?

God forgives him.

That's a whole lot of sin for one of God's favorites. That's a whole lot of sin for anybody. But in the end, David, God's "beloved," shows us that God longs for us to confess our sins. God wants to show us mercy. And even when we get power hungry and lost, if we take responsibility for our sins and ask God for forgiveness, He forgives.

John Nieder and Thomas M. Thompson, in *Forgive and Love Again,* discuss word pictures of forgiveness in the Bible. "To forgive is to sandblast a wall of graffiti, leaving it looking like new."[7] You've seen cartoon drawings and loops of the florescent paint on the dirty cement. When you forgive, it's polished clean.

Nieder and Thompson go on to say, "To forgive is to smash a clay pot into a thousand pieces so it can never be pieced together again."[8] Like the glass that leapt from your hands and shattered on the floor, when you forgive, the shards are too small to be glued together. The tiny pieces must be swept up and thrown away.

Forgiveness isn't an add-on when justice has been completely served. Forgiveness is an ongoing process and a choice.

Let's Get Practical

How can you become generous with forgiveness? Read on.

In Your Home

- **Talk when you are angry.** Often issues get blown out of proportion because we try to stuff our feelings. Talk about your hurts now, and teach your kids to do the same.
- **Write your apology, even to your kids.** A short note left on the counter or in their bedroom packs big meaning. Kids need to see us address our mistakes.

- **Apologize often.** We need to model the behavior we hope to see in our children. It sounds silly to say kids need to be taught to apologize, but it's true.

In Your Community

- **Let go of the annoying.** Bad drivers, the rude checkout girl, and the neighbor who refuses to wave. Finding ways to let go of little offenses help prepare us for dealing with offenses on a larger scale.
- **Read *Amish Grace: How Forgiveness Transcended Tragedy* with friends.**
- **Make peace with your coworker—the one who knows how to work your nerves.** I know it's tough. She would annoy me too.

In The World

- **Look to others.** Stories inspire me to act. The Forgiveness Project, http://theforgivenessproject.com/, shares real-life narratives (over 160 at this time) written by people around the world who have experienced various atrocities. The Forgiveness Project also pushes people to explore forgiveness in new and real ways.
- **Pray for those who don't deserve it.** Pray for individuals who commit the unthinkable and leaders who hurt in the name of power. Stop. Notice names and pray forgiveness.

Dinner Table Dialogue

- Discuss the mistakes you have made, a person you have hurt, and how the situation was resolved.
- Why do you think people refuse to apologize? What are some of the consequences of holding back and refusing to apologize?

- When is the last time you apologized? Discuss the situation and the response of the person you apologized to.
- Come up with alternative ways of saying "I'm sorry." Examples: "I wish I wouldn't have said that. I didn't realize I was being hurtful. Can we have a do-over?"

One Last Point to Drive It Home

You are forgiving and good, O Lord, abounding in love to all who call to you (Psalm 86:5). Jesus' sole purpose for walking the earth was so that we can be forgiven.

CHAPTER 7

GENEROUS WITH TIME

Everything in Life Doesn't Need an App

I used to think to be generous with time, you needed to have time. Now I think that in order to be generous with time you need to find time, tackle it, tie it up with a rope, and protect it.

I would rather give you fifty dollars than fifty minutes. This proves a small problem, since I usually lack both.

To get fifty dollars, I fill in a couple of times for my friend who tutors, write an article for a kids' magazine on bats (random but true), or sell off bins of clothes that no longer fit my kids. To get fifty minutes, I drop one of the thirty plates I keep spinning, feel guilty, spend the rest of the day sweeping up the pieces of whatever I dropped, and silently curse myself for not having a third hand to keep it all going.

In order to be generous with time, our family needed to find time. It went missing somewhere around 2000, and that elusive thing hasn't been seen in over a decade. In order to find time, we needed to learn how to rest.

See, when the world screams, "Better, faster, more!" not only do I comply, but I attempt to improve the "better, faster, more" mentality. (I'm a go-getter like that.)

Thankfully, to help us manage our busyness and free up time, many must-have applications have been developed:

- An app allowing you to staple an imaginary piece of paper. As if you could replace the joy of actual stapling!

- An app rating your sexual performance. No joke here, people.
- An app for blowing out your birthday candles. Who has time for candles?
- An app claiming to help you regenerate hair follicles. I'm not sure how this works. Are you required to rub the electronic device on your head?
- An app that allows you to throw a pretend piece of paper at a pretend teacher. Will the fun never end?

As I scroll over page after page of applications designed to assist and entertain, I acknowledge our precious time is being sucked up faster than I can "accidently" vacuum up Polly Pocket clothing.

With weeks of movies and must-see episodes on our DVR, it's easy to check out. Plus, Netflix allows us a quick fix when the DVR just doesn't hold what we are in the mood for.

The need for more time isn't new.

I remember waiting, hands clenched and body tense, for Mr. Wartella, my third grade teacher, to utter the one word I dreaded most . . . "Go!" Timed multiplication tests sent me spinning. Sure, zeroes through fives proved easy, but the sixes? Oh, those terrible sixes. Mastering the sixes kept me away from what I deeply desired—my golden star.

You see, Mr. Wartella awarded stars each time a student mastered a level of multiplication facts. After a level was mastered, students placed their precious stars on the wall for everyone to "ooh" and "ah" about. However, my tiny row stopped, and I stayed locked in the sixes' box while the rest of the class sped toward those daunting twelves.

Regardless of how much I practiced at home, when the timed test started, instead of filling in answers quickly, I froze. I sat quietly, and I wished for more time. If I just had ten more seconds, I knew mastering my sixes and placing a star sticker into my box was within reach.

The days of sitting in a small orange chair, willing myself to produce more and better, are now gone, but the same concept still rings true to my life today. I race or sometimes I freeze, but the clock still taunts me.

And honestly, when I'm not racing and going and producing, I feel a little anxiety bubbling, like there is something I am forgetting to do. I feel like everyone is one lap ahead of me, and I'm standing at the starting line wondering what exactly I'm supposed to do in this race. The 86,400 seconds we hold in our little hands every day just don't do it for me.

It wasn't enough in third grade, and it's not enough now.

If We Could Only Live the Simple Life

For the past few years, there's been a movement to simplify. Sick of feeling ragged and drained, people recognize the need to slow the pace of life.

This Simplicity Movement is great in theory—with theory being images I've conjured up in my head. When I picture the simple life, I envision living in a faraway cabin secluded from life's distractions. At our rustic cabin, you'd find me plucking homegrown vegetables off the vine and hanging a colorful array of handmade clothes outside to dry. Shane would be whittling, and our kids would be playing jacks on the front porch. Our life would be slow—our way of rebelling against society's rushed pace. See, if I lived in the log cabin, I would have more time. More time to do for others and connect with God.

But ready to burst my log cabin dream is someone who actually lives in a log cabin—Brandee.

"I'm sitting in my own log cabin in the sticks and trust and believe, Sister, God isn't here anymore than He is anywhere else. Also, it's very chaotic up here with Wonder Pets and Pop-Tart snacks."

Shoot.

I guess those photos of the simple life are illusions. Curse you, simplicity bloggers, with your art-like photographs and your homemade jam. I really wanted my husband to learn how to whittle.

The Bible Mandates Rest, Which Means Find a Way to Rest

To make issues with time and busyness worse, the Bible goes to great lengths to communicate that rest is not a suggestion but a mandate.

Verses pop from the pages.

> *Remember the Sabbath day by keeping it holy. Six days you shall labor and do all your work, but the seventh day is a Sabbath to the Lord your God. On it you shall not do any work, neither you, nor your son or daughter, nor your male or female servant, nor your animals, nor any foreigner residing in your towns. For in six days the Lord made the heavens and the earth, the sea, and all that is in them, but he rested on the seventh day. Therefore the Lord blessed the Sabbath day and made it holy.* (Exodus 20:8-11)

Rest. God rested, and our family needed rest.

> *Then, because so many people were coming and going that they did not even have a chance to eat, he said to them, "Come with me by yourselves to a quiet place and get some rest."* (Mark 6:31)

I skip meals all the time in the name of productivity, but what I really need is rest. God instructed His disciples to rest. I am His disciple, so I need to rest.

Then, we have the following verse, which should have said, "Amy, heads-up, this one is for you."

> *In vain you rise early and stay up late, toiling for food to eat—for he grants sleep to those he loves. (Psalm 127:2)*

Translation: my constant producing is in vain.

God knows I work full-time, raise kids, dote on the husband, attempt to be a good friend, write, run family places, and exercise. He doesn't care. God wants me to rest. He needs me to stop making time an idol I refuse to release. He won't bless my manic toiling unless I rest, and I will not have time to share with others if I do not learn to rest.

And So the Sullivans Rested

It was one night in late fall when we were scheduled to be three
different places (all in the name of good). This is when I broke.
I texted the class mom to let her know I wasn't bringing treats,
no-showed a meeting, missed a writing deadline, skipped a
jump rope performance, ditched carpooling for basketball,
and proceeded to drown my sorrows in two bowls of Cream of
Wheat. When my eyes quit stinging and the snot cleared, my
husband and I decided two things.

Fabulous Idea #1: Unplugged Night

One evening a week we unplugged from all things electronic.

Fabulous Idea #2: Stay at Home Day

We committed to nothing on Saturdays and stayed home.
Unable to ditch all of our obligations, we carved time where we
could.

What came from Fabulous Ideas #1 and #2? You'd be sur-
prised. Instead of feeling as if we were missing out on life, we
felt as if we grabbed ahold of it. We remained in control, and
instead of becoming control freaks—which is absolutely in my
nature—we offered a handful of time to God.

Two weeks into our fabulous ideas (which means only four
days of "resting"), the craziest thing happened. God deepened
the relationships with the people who lined our lives. By being available, opportunities to serve others flew into our paths.
Occasions which were natural. Opportunities we didn't have to
schedule or come up with on our own.

We had no idea we were missing out on quality time with
our neighbors and friends, not to mention our kids! A little
obvious to the world, maybe, but missing from our brains was
the fact that all of our running our kids around wasn't actually

"quality time." (To see activities which constitute kid-approved family time, read *Dear Parents* in the back.)

Sound bites heard from the Sullivans while spending time with our kids:

"Get in the car. Hurry up, hurry … up!"

"Wait, go back in the house."

"We need to run home. We forgot your basketball shoes."

"Not your old basketball shoes! I meant your new basketball shoes. Get your new shoes!"

"Crap! I thought you performed next Tuesday."

"You forgot your backpack at the dance studio? How are you supposed to finish your illustrated timeline on the history of North Carolina?"

"I'm NOT driving fast."

Protect Your Time

By allowing space in our lives, we leave room for the opportunities God cooks up for us. If we quit plowing through life, God's agenda becomes more important than ours, and He surprises us in ways we can't fathom, ways that don't make sense.

Think of good ole Sarah getting pregnant at age ninety. Surprise! (Genesis 21:2)

And what about Mary, who was happily planning her wedding? And then *bam*! She found herself pregnant with our Lord and Savior. Wow! (Luke 1:28)

These people accepted God's surprises—and what *goodness* they discovered.

God uses people who are open and receptive, and if we aren't open and receptive—if we don't protect our time—we miss out.

I don't want to miss out. No way.

Let's Get Practical

What's the best way to spend your time? Be intentional. Don't allow your days to become filled with the meaningless.

Your Home

- **Create intentional down time.** Dear Amy: Resist the urge to fill up your free minutes. Dear Everyone Else: This applies to you too.
- **Carve out a small amount of time each day (I'm talking ten minutes) when your entire family does their own thing, quietly.** Then, honor that time, which means do not answer the phone, answer the text, or answer your children. Seriously, this is good for them. You regain sanity. Your kids start to understand setting boundaries in regard to time.
- **Write out a list of how you spend your time daily.** Evaluate it. Are you pleased with where your time and energy are going?

Your Community

- **Pick up five pieces of trash on your next trip to the park, and ask your kids to do the same.** My hubby likes to take the kids to do this on the frontage road by our neighborhood.
- **Invite your new neighbor to go with you on your next walk.** Hello, exercise and girl time? Bonus.
- **Learn Exodus 16:29 and then make time the topic of conversation.** Chat it up with people in your circles and pray this verse for them.

The World

- **Consider taking a mission trip or a service vacation.**
- **Watch a documentary.** What do you know about Burma or North Korea? Many documentaries can be viewed for free.
- **They wrote it, so don't just throw it in the bill basket.**

Those organizations you support write you letters. Read them, and hey, write back!

Dinner Table Dialogue

- What is your favorite way to spend family time? Least favorite?
- What is an activity you currently participate in that you view as a time-suck and would like to cut out? Why are you hesitant to cut it out?
- What is an activity in which you spend time trying to better your community? The world?

CHAPTER 8

GENEROUS WITH PRAYER
Why You Should Wait for the Enchiladas

I used to think prayer wasn't active. Now I know it lives, breathes, and changes lives.

I never really prayed until I thought my daughter could die.

I looked at a baby girl I only recently met and planned out her life. She'll play tennis like me and shrug off life's problems like her dad. She'll wear pigtails for her kindergarten pictures, and she'll love books, especially *Brown Bear* by Eric Carle.

Looking back at home videos, I can see something was wrong then, but as a new mom, I saw nothing strange about my wiggly newborn.

Parenting books give details about sleep patterns, temperatures, shot schedules, and growth charts. Parenting books don't tell you how to handle blue babies.

While doing dishes, I looked down and saw my daughter swinging in the portable swing, but she was blue. I snatched her from her swing, and I ran to the window so I could see her in the light. Blue.

I closed my eyes tightly and then quickly opened them again. Still blue.

I fled to the hospital. Gripping the steering wheel, I forced myself to look at the street and fill my head with things other than a blue baby.

Red light. Stop.

Go faster.

Signal, pass.

Straight.

Turn.

Emergency Room Entrance.

As days passed at the hospital, my thinking remained choppy. I broke down every task into steps because even simple thoughts overwhelmed me. Phrases and short sentences cluttered my head. I don't remember showering. I know I didn't eat.

Days. Ticked. On.

Answers were hidden. Doctors seemed too busy. The hospital room remained dark, even during the day. I didn't want it light anyway.

Eventually, they labeled my daughter's breathing problems: Neuroendocrine Cell Hyperplasia. She would need oxygen twenty-four hours a day indefinitely. Best-case scenario: full-time oxygen for five years. Worst-case scenario: chronic lung problems for life.

I prayed eyes-burning-snot-slinging kinds of prayers. I cried and cursed, and then something happened—something I never deemed possible, something others did every day, but something I never saw myself capable of.

I quit.

I had never quit anything in my life, but right there in the dark hospital room, I quit praying. I didn't stop hoping my daughter would get better, but I quit asking God. I was too tired. I ran out of words. There was nothing new to say.

I refused to speak to God. He was getting the silent treatment in a major way. If things didn't change, He could get it forever. When anyone spoke even a hint of God-talk, I envisioned myself plugging my ears and yelling, "La, la, la! I can't hear you!"

I heard stories of mothers who prayed years, decades, and even a lifetime for their sick children, but not me. No, I couldn't even make it eleven days. I sucked as a prayer. And, even worse, as a mother.

At this point, I learned about prayer. Not from anything I did or the way God revealed Himself to me, but I learned about prayer by the way others took over in pleas and petitions for our sick daughter.

When I gave up, those closest to me rallied. Will and Lindy brought peanut butter sandwiches, and Wendy brought lattes. Krista cleaned my bathroom, and Leah brought a whispered version of "Happy Birthday." The Greshams and Austins showed up at our house, and Tina showed up for the tests.

Friends rallied to meet our physical needs, and then friends fought our feelings of defeat with prayer, and they didn't quit.

Our community gave us the best gift, one we couldn't muster ourselves: hope and prayer.

This would be a nice little story if it ended there, but our daughter's health did not completely improve for over three-and-a-half years. Three-and-a-half years of full-time oxygen, hospital stays, and doctors' appointments. Three-and-a-half years of sleepless nights. Three-and-a-half years of people who refused to stop praying, and after our daughter was healed, those same people celebrated with us with thanksgiving and a "Hooray, you are off oxygen!" cake (We love you, Stars).

That's what prayer does. It carries people who don't have the strength to stand on their own.

When You Don't Love Praying

For years, I didn't enjoy prayer. True prayer was a discipline I reserved for those I viewed as big-time Christians. Clearly not me, and clearly not a privilege.

My prayer life consisted of the five minutes in between coffee and getting dressed in the morning. I considered a solid quiet time whatever hopes I jammed into my spare five or six minutes in the morning. I scribbled requests into a bound journal and peppered my prayers with words of thanks and accolades for the Creator, but prayer did not come naturally, and I wasn't good at it.

My prayer life contained massive holes, and I wasn't sure what was missing or how to fix it. But I love words—always have—and when I got serious about prayer, I fixated on two things: the rosary and good advice.

Yep, the rosary. It's a secret I keep close. It's one of the Catholic practices I still honor. I own an old plastic rosary from my grandmother, and as I pray, I know she prayed the same way, on the same rosary. And there's comfort in that.

As a former Catholic girl, I like the way the round beads slip through my fingers, each bead embedded with meaning. *The Apostle's Creed, Glory Be, Our Father,* three *Hail Marys,* and I'm off. Praying the same way as millions today and the millions before me.

Have you ever sat in a huge stadium, looked around, and became knocked-off-your-feet overwhelmed by the sheer presence of each person in each seat being at the exact same spot for the exact same reason as you? That's how I feel when I pray the rosary: united with a group, not alone.

The rosary keeps my scattered and undisciplined mind focused and helps me fight off thoughts about the next episode of *The Tonight Show with Jimmy Fallon* or stops me from worrying if the bright-blue nail polish on my toes is too bright (not too bright, never too bright).

Don't get me wrong. Praying the rosary isn't the only way I pray. I've long departed from uttering only formulated prayers. I know God doesn't require a scripted prayer. His deepest desire is for us to converse with Him. And when conversing, I don't need the presence of beads, but I like them anyway. They help keep me focused.

Next to the rosary, good advice also jumpstarted my prayer life. Grab your highlighter for this one. Here it is:

If you are praying, you aren't doing it wrong.

These words changed me.

The Message says it well:

> *God's Spirit is right alongside helping us along. If we don't know how or what to pray, it doesn't matter. He does our praying in and for us, making prayer out of our wordless sighs, our aching groans. He knows us far better than we know ourselves. (Romans: 8:27-28a)[1]*

Even if my prayers for others were simple and selfish, God would teach me and shake me up through them, and He did.

This means praying in the car is great. Praying while doing dishes is fantastic. Praying about the hiccups in life is right on. Praying for the too big and out of reach is perfect. Ongoing prayer as conversation is exactly what He desires.

I should have put this chapter first, because it's the most valuable thing we can do for others.

My friend, Alene, says we overlook prayer as a way of serving others because we don't see immediate results, and we'd rather be actively "doing something."

She's right. What's prayer when there's action to be had? Prayer seems stagnant.

Maybe it's because when we pray, we don't move. Therefore, we feel our cries don't impact.

Crazy, right? Tsk, tsk. I know better, and you do too.

With prayer, we can serve others in the early morning or the middle of the night. We don't need to schedule time or worry about interrupting lives. Prayer is a way we can give again and again.

Think of Your Prayer Life as the Food Pantry

It is ten minutes before dinner, and my kids won't stop bugging me. I'm making their favorite—enchiladas—if they will only be patient. They want top-shelf treats. I want them to leave me alone. They need to let me finish the delicious meal they don't even know they want, because all they see is the tasty-but-out-of-reach treats.

Kid: Mom, can I have licorice?

Me: Nope.

Kid: Chips?

Me: No.

Kid: A healthy snack?

Me: Oh, you are desperate. No.

Kid: What about a fruit bar? It's not even for me. It's for Auburn. She says they got home late, and she didn't eat lunch.

Me: No. Tell Auburn she can eat dinner with us in ten minutes.

Kid: What about these crackers? I think they are stale.

Me: Noooooooo. Goooooooo.

I know if my kids eat a bunch of junk-o-la, they won't want anything to do with the nutritious goodness that's just about ready to hit the table. This illustration makes me think of our never-ending pleas to God. Asking, asking, asking but not fully understanding the possibilities that await us (or others we love like poor, starving Auburn who hasn't even had lunch!).

I think God feels the same way. We are the kids begging for junk food because we can't see the opportunities God has planned. Although He is pleased we rely on Him for what is out of our reach, He's not about to give us licorice or stale crackers.

This example also makes me think that although I'm annoyed by my children's constant chatter regarding what they think they need, I am also pleased they ask for it.

Are you following me on this whole analogy, or am I totally off base? Are you left wondering just what makes my enchiladas so amazing? God wants us to ask and ask and ask for ourselves and for others, and He wants us to keep asking when He doesn't give us what we want.

Answered Prayers

Two-year-old Gore drowned in an irrigation ditch—but didn't. Congenital Cystic Adenomatoid Malformation threatened Gage, but he beat it. A former homeless woman is given a car, and she uses it to transport women to church. The unemployed dad of four gets the job over those more qualified. A couple who despises each other falls in love again.

Answers to prayers.

During each of these events, I know people who called out to God for mercy. People who prayed for situations most deemed hopeless. People who wouldn't give up on a miracle and served others with prayer.

Lessons on Praying for Others from Those in the Bible

Pray for those you know need encouragement, even if they are strangers: Paul

Roman, Pharisee, persecutor of Christians, champion of Jesus. To look at a map of Paul's travels makes me dizzy. I drive in my car to the early-morning service at church and get tired. Paul circles Middle-Eastern Europe for years and never loses the drive to continue.

Paul prays unceasingly for strangers in a strange land. He thanks God for people he doesn't know, and he prays there will be a time he can visit them in person so he can be an encouragement to them.

> *First, I thank my God through Jesus Christ for all of you, because your faith is being reported all over the world. God, whom I serve with my whole heart in preaching the gospel of his Son is my witness how constantly I remember you in my prayers at all times.* (Romans 1:8a)

Pray for compassion for your people: Moses

Those whiny Israelites seriously considered returning to Egypt because—even though God led them out of slavery— quail, manna, and water weren't enough.

> *The Israelites said to them, "If only we had died by the Lord's hand in Egypt! There we sat around pots of meat and ate all the food we wanted, but you have brought us out into this desert to starve this entire assembly to death." (Exodus 16:3)*

They struggled to follow God's instructions. Therefore, they wandered and wandered and well, you get it. Moses prays for God to show compassion to His people.

Psalm 90 smacks of goodness. The whole thing, but big-time focus on 90:13.

> *Relent, O Lord! How long will it be? Have compassion on your servants.*

Pray for forgiveness: Jesus

Jesus said, "Father, forgive them for they do not know what they are doing." And they divided up his clothes by casting lots. (Luke 23:34)

It's the whole story. All of it.

Jesus' prayer of forgiveness for an undeserving people. When He could have cursed us, He prayed.

I can't pretend to understand, but I can try to follow His example.

Let's Get Practical

Dinner Table Dialogue is vital in this chapter. Why? Because it's in simple dinner conversation where you learn about the needs in your home, family, and the world. Here we go.

In Your Home

- **Create a prayer ring.** My friend, Kathi, saves old Christmas cards, hole punches the cards in the upper left-hand corner, and then connects the cards with a small, metal ring. Her family leaves the cards in a basket next to the dinner table and takes turns flipping each card and praying for different families during dinner.

- **Display a prayer board.** Use a large wipe board or chalkboard with the name of a person your family is committed to praying for during the week. Allow your kids to help choose the person you are highlighting, and change it weekly.

- **Prayer walk through your neighborhood.** Not only is the praying good, but the more we are outside, the more we are inclined to interact with people.

In Your Community

- **Pray for church and community leaders by name.** Make it a point to help your children learn the names of people in your church and your community.
- **Begin a prayer group for the local school.** As a former teacher, I've seen the impact these groups can have in schools and in building relationships with parents and teachers. Oh, and after you pray, bring the teachers treats.
- **Prayer walk past and around your community's main buildings and up and down its streets.** A group of friends and I did this. You start off feeling crazy, but you end up excited.

In The World

- **Make friends with an international college student, a coworker, or someone from a different country.** Get to know new people and discover needs from around the world you never even knew about.
- **Dig out a map.** Pick a region of the world and research it with your kids and pray for the needs of the country.
- **Pay attention to labels on your clothing.** When you get dressed, flip the tag and pray for the people within the country in which it was made.

Dinner Table Dialogue

- Have ongoing conversations about answered prayer.
- Have your family discuss the needs they have, and pray for them together.
- Just as you teach your kids the names of people in your church and community, make an effort to learn the names of your children's friends. Knowing names of your children's friends and their siblings and parents makes it easier to pray for specific needs.

CHAPTER 9

GENEROUS WITH MONEY
Ouch! It Hurts!

"I used to think giving money was an obligation. Now I think financial generosity is addicting, like getting tattoos. Um, that's just what I heard, Mom."

After a moving sermon on "stuff," I felt the need to do something for someone else. I wanted to give to someone I didn't know. I wanted to do it in a way where I expected nothing in return. I e-mailed my pastor about a person or family we could help financially. Of course, he knew of just the person. Our pastor said to forget about Christmas; this person would have difficulty making it through the week. Her name was Kendra (obviously, I changed her name), and she came from what he called a "challenged" background. Regardless, whenever transportation was available, she attended church, trying to steer herself a different direction. Our pastor suggested a food card to a local grocery store, and I promised it would happen by the end of the week.

It was a busy week. First, out-of-town company was coming in for the holidays, so I needed to get the house in holiday shape, which meant cleaning, cooking, a little more decorating, and, of course, more wrapping. I'd get the gift card the next time I stopped at the store.

Then, as an annual tradition, a close friend and her daughter came over to make cookies, and I had to buy ingredients and find new and yummy recipes to offer up.

After this, a big winter storm descended. Thick, heavy snow covered the ground. It was the kind of snow I remember from childhood memories in Northern Michigan. Our family built snowmen, went sledding, and sat around our fireplace. I needed to get to the store for that gift card, but it kept snowing and blowing. After fourteen inches, the power went out. You sure couldn't go to the grocery store in that kind of weather. So, our family wrapped more presents by candlelight.

My company arrived in the dark, and we celebrated Christmas with grandparents who love to spoil. The power soon came on, but instead of going to the grocery store for the gift card, we decided to go downtown. After all, my family was only here for two days. Everything was still snow-covered, but the plows were running and roads would be fine to drive on. We went to a specialty chocolate lounge, drank up liquid truffles, and feasted on thick, rich brownies. Then we decided we were hungry for something more than dessert, so we went to this hip Mexican restaurant notorious for to-die-for guacamole prepared right at your table.

I totally forgot about the gift card.

The next day my company left, and after a final inspection of the gifts, we decided our girls needed a couple more gifts. We capped our spending, but because our oldest changed her wish list, we were officially getting her nothing she wanted. Can't have that! Off to the store, but not for a gift card.

Christmas Eve arrived. Our tree sparkled. Our house smelled of cinnamon. Our refrigerator burst with food. I sent my husband to the store for the gift card, and I called Kendra. It would be most convenient for me to give her the card at Christmas Eve Service. Never mind that she couldn't use the card because the store would be closed. And forget about the fact that the store would also be closed the following day since it was Christmas, so using it then would be out of the question too. I hoped she wouldn't mind.

Problem: Kendra couldn't get to the service because she didn't have transportation. Sigh. How annoying. I wrote directions to her apartment and offered to drop off the gift card before we went to church.

Important fact: I didn't offer her a ride to church because well, our jeep doesn't really have room, and if we took her, we'd also have to bring her home, and since she lived downtown it was actually the opposite way from where we were headed, and come on, it was Christmas Eve.

After putting my girls in matching velvet Christmas dresses and staring at my knock-off Banana Republic bracelet for an endless amount of time, we loaded up the family to do some good and visit Kendra. However, loading up the jeep took a little longer than expected. My eldest was whiney, my youngest was crying, my husband was less than excited about making an extra stop, and I was distracted because church was sure to be crowded, and there wouldn't be anywhere to sit, because now we were officially late.

We found Kendra's apartment. Darkness filled her ground-level window. I felt terrible. What if they didn't have power?

I took off my ankle-length leather coat, because it was much too fancy to deliver gift cards in. A light went on—*Oh good, she did have power*—and Kendra poked her head out of the door. She was younger than I expected, and she invited my husband and me in. We left the girls outside in the car. This would just take a minute, and we didn't know these people. Of course, we didn't want them to meet our kids.

This is what I remember from the whole interaction: The apartment reeked of smoke while ashtrays and poker chips lined the coffee table. There wasn't a hint of Christmas anywhere, and Kendra shouted in a you-better-get-your-butt-out-here tone of voice to her fiancé to wake up. Kendra thanked us for the gift card because it had been difficult since she had lost her job at the Veteran's Hospital, but she knew it would get better because God would provide.

"Yes, siree, God would provide!" I echoed as I stared down at that gorgeous knock-off bracelet. I loved that thing! It really would go with just about any outfit. Oh yeah, we needed to go because we were late for church. "Merry Christmas!"

As we were driving away, I had a nagging feeling something was wrong. Maybe I should have wrapped up some of those leftover Christmas cookies for them. Nah, there really weren't that many left. What was that weird feeling I was having? Oh, now I know—they have our phone number. I hope they don't call us for money.

Blah.

More compassion happens at banks' drive-thru windows.

Would you believe months passed before I figured out the nagging feeling I couldn't shake was God?

Thinking back on this whole interaction makes me uncomfortable, but then the idea of money in general makes me uncomfortable. So, as you can deduce, the idea of giving money makes me, well, uncomfortable.

Your Thoughts (and Mine) on Money

I intentionally saved this chapter until the end of the book.

No one likes to talk about money. Most of us feel as if we don't have enough money. Sure, sure. Compared to the world's standards, we are rich. But when the car needs new tires, the dog needs shots, and the hot water heater breaks, we feel as though serving others by being generous with money isn't an option.

How does giving money make you feel? In the book *The Power of Giving*, authors Jamal and McKinnon discuss the attitude many of us have toward money.

"You likely have a complex set of emotions attached to money, emotions that drive many of your life decisions—where you work, what you do with your money, and even if your marriage will survive."[1]

Jamal and McKinnon go on to tell about a workshop McKinnon led on money. He asked the audience to think back to their childhood and pinpoint some of their first memories of money and the feelings attached to these memories.

I didn't really like this idea, but I tried it. What were my first memories of money? What is my attitude toward money today?

As a child, changing schools yearly became more of an expected routine than a surprise. New buses, teachers, routines, people, and unwritten social rules to learn. Never knowing when the next move would come, I remained ready.

Good schools were safe places I wanted to stay even after the bell rang. Places like Washington Elementary School, where reading well and behaving earned you rewards, such as colorful and shiny beads on your behavior necklace, plus smiles and extra attention from teachers.

Bad schools were places I walked into and held my breath most of the day, hoping no one would notice me. Places like Troy Junior High, where ownership of multiple Swatch watches would earn you a coveted spot at the cool table, and the wrong shoes could get you ostracized permanently.

I grew up in a small town in Northern Michigan, and the world of "mean girls" shocked me. As a sixth grader in Michigan, I still lined up to go from class to class. I had a desk to keep my pencil box in and a little hook for my jacket. I held a place in the top reading group, participated in sports, maintained solid friendships, and slept every night with a Pound Puppy named KC.

When my mom dropped me off at the office of Troy Junior High, and a much-too-busy secretary handed me a schedule and ushered me out of the office, I knew my world had changed. In the school of 1,200-plus students, I carried around every book from every class for weeks because lockers baffled me. Teachers seemed put-out by yet another student to teach. No one noticed my classes were too easy, and I learned if you were quiet, teachers didn't care if you actually did your assignment or not. Kids were mean, and friends were anyone who didn't make fun of you—at least not to your face. I still slept with KC, but I knew he was headed for a box in the closet.

We didn't have money. I knew this, so I made a point not to require much.

It was at this time in my life I justified the if-you-need-it-you-could-steal-it policy. I knew stealing was wrong. However, stealing something I needed didn't seem *as* wrong. It started with purses, make-up, and trinkets. It exploded to owning nine bathing suits at one time.

I equated money with stability, and since neither seemed within my reach, I decided to find each on my own. As I grew up, the theme of money and not having enough was consistent. Even when I had everything I needed, the what-ifs haunted me.

After I married, my husband and I earned enough to pay the bills and save. Life felt good, stable. Then, when our doctors diagnosed our daughter with a lung disease our world stopped, but the mailman continued to deliver bills.

I quit my job and spent most of my time at the hospital or locked in our townhouse panicking over every sneeze.

My husband almost quit his last semester of grad school. Even with insurance, we watched our tiny savings vanish during our first few days in the hospital.

We moved to a different part of the state. A place where the housing was cheap and friends were scarce. Good-bye supportive community. Hello attempting to make friends in awkward ways, such as throwing myself at the children's librarian, pretending I enjoy running, and yelling out to a teenage mom walking her child.

For six months, we paid both a mortgage at our old townhome and rent at a new townhome. By the first of the month, every month, we were already 600 dollars in debt, and we hadn't paid a single bill or bought food.

I prided myself on making an entire meal, which yielded leftovers, for less than five dollars.

Amy's Homemade Pot Pie (Poverty Style)

•	Frozen pie crust	$1.00
•	Can of chicken gravy	$1.00
•	Frozen bag of veggies	$1.00
•	1 chicken breast	$1.50-ish

Random Cheap Meat and Stewed Tomatoes

- Cheap Mystery Meat $3.50
- Stewed tomatoes $1.00
- Unused veggies from the previous meal. $0

Yeah, yeah. Maybe not a picture of healthy eating, but I can go like this all day. Loaded baked potatoes (this means cheese and butter), about six versions of breakfast, and anything with dry beans and tortillas.

Shane grumbled and said I would have enjoyed the Great Depression. I shrugged and patted myself on the back for spending less than forty dollars a week on groceries. Once, while walking to the park (favorite free activity), I found a five-dollar bill. I bawled. Later in the week, someone stole our cheap umbrella stroller, and I bawled again. I also snuck into the shady thief's backyard and stole that bad boy back. Do *not* mess with my favorite free activity. (Remind me to tell you this story if we meet. It involves me running with a baby and an oxygen tank into a gated back yard with barking dogs.) I'm sort of like Jason Bourne.

We now understood the words *working poor.*

When I wasn't busy thinking up delicious and notorious gourmet concoctions, I spent my days worrying, which was pretty much all the time. My biggest issue, insecurity with money, sat in my lap. Ugly and loud, it demanded my attention daily.

You will never rise above this, my insecurity taunted.

Your daughter is getting worse, and you can't afford her treatment, insecurity continued.

When Generosity Helps You Learn About Money

Every day I calculated how much debt we accrued each month. Full of pride, we struggled to tell people about our financial situation. And emotionally, we pretty much sat on empty.

Meet Heath and Loraine.

We met Heath and Loraine upon first moving to Denver. As newlyweds, Loraine and I had each prayed for a friend since we arrived in Colorado, only to meet later at church and realize we shared a wall in our apartment building. If I knocked on my wall, she heard it.

The Ericksons are also lifetime friends—the kinds who know every nasty detail about you and yet still love you. My husband and I celebrated Christmases, college graduations, and the joys and holes of everyday life with them in our first years of marriage.

However, life moved the Ericksons back to Wisconsin, and the miles separated us. Through this time, we stayed in touch, and it was at one of my darkest cry-on-the-dirty-linoleum-kitchen-floor moments when Loraine called and asked for the name and address of our doctor.

Heath and Loraine sold a house, and they wanted to help us out—with a single check, they did. See, the Ericksons decided on a certain amount of money to give us, and although they were completely unaware, it was the exact amount we owed a local doctor.

A tiny spark of faith started to burn.

Next up, John and Steph.

John and Steph asked us over for dinner. After dinner, they told us we looked tired, as if we could use a break. With a few kind words, they shared a check with us.

Before us sat a couple who needed the money they were giving to us. Not only giving, but seriously thrilled about giving. *Wait, had they been drinking?* It didn't make sense, and yet, it made perfect sense.

So we cried, and they cried, and we took the check because that's part of giving too—being able to receive.

Another confirmation God provided.

Neither couple knew it, but giving so freely at a time when our family needed it formed my ideas on giving (even if I didn't know how to put those ideas into actions yet).

Seeing a need and unselfishly giving. Sure, rich people gave money, but normal people? Did people really embody the idea behind the whole widow-and-mite story? Giving extravagant sums of money that would actually be missed? (Luke 21:1-4)

Apparently so.

But the monetary gifts didn't stop there.

A large check from my college roommate's mother showed up in our mailbox. My dad sent money. My mom sent money. My sister sent money. My faraway aunt sent money. It wasn't just money, either. People provided in other ways. The Allens took us on vacation when we couldn't afford to leave our house, let alone the state.

People covered us in generosity.

I'm Not Going to Tell You How to Spend Your Money, But . . .

Entire aisles of books have been written on the topic of God's ideas surrounding money. Therefore, I will not tell you why you need to give money to others. (Hello … You bought this book. My hunch is you already know.) Instead, I want to share tips on smart giving (wisdom you may need). I'm not talking about smart giving as it relates to people.

This section touches on smart giving as it applies to organized establishments.

Maybe it's because someone broke into my car, twice.

Or maybe it's because, in college, the police showed up at my house to arrest my roommate who, to my surprise, had been involved in a variety of no-good activities around campus.

Or maybe it's because I used to live in the city, and I punched a code to get into my parking area, and a code to get into my apartment gate, and a code to get to my apartment building door. Then, I unlocked my building's door. After this, I proceeded to unlock two locks on my apartment door. All before entering my home.

Or maybe it's because I used to spend my days with smooth-talking, at-risk teens.

Whatever the reason, I tend to be not-so-trusting when it comes to money and giving. See, after friends and family rallied to support us for years, there was no denying we wanted to bless others the same way. But when it came to supporting organizations, I wanted to show savvy.

I think it's irresponsible to write a check just because you watched a video with moving images and a rocking soundtrack. I believe God wants us to be smart givers.

6 Tips to Assist You in Smart Giving

- **Stalk (in a totally non-creepy way).** Follow the organization on social media. If candy bars and coffee distributors have Facebook and Twitter accounts, my guess is the place you want to support has one too. Read updates and tweets in order to better familiarize yourself.
- **Show me the money.** Look for transparency. How is money spent, and can donors obtain quick access to documents on spending?
- **Find an organization you believe in and stick with it.** I bet you can spout off names of dozens of organizations providing worthy services. With one quick search on Google, I discovered a list of over thirty anti-human trafficking organizations. Are you interested in the fight against poverty? Too many choices turn us into here-and-there givers. If you want to make an impact, don't spread out your giving.
- **Start a conversation and get the dirt.** This takes effort, but toss out questions to your friends and the online world about past experiences with the organization you want to support.
- **Give locally.** You know the people. You know the services they provide. You can even schedule a tour to observe what's happening.
- **Research.** Take a peek at guides designed to rate charities. (Check out the *Let's Get Practical* section.)

Because Kids Just Get It

My daughter earned thirty cents by folding laundry, a chore she despises. Then she walked up to a beautiful little girl in a wheelchair, pulled the change from her red, paisley purse, and handed the girl's mom two dimes and ten pennies.

"This is to help you with her," she offered.

And when I heard, I wanted to drop down on the church's tiled floor with embarrassment. I worried about offending.

But as my daughter sat on a folding chair in an overcrowded sanctuary and created a happy face from watermelon and blueberries instead of eating her lunch, I began to think Matthew was right. *I tell you the truth, unless you change and become like little children, you will never enter the kingdom of Heaven* (Matthew 18:3).

Let's look for moments like this. Moments we don't see coming, but they show up.

Let's Get Practical

There are many reasons people hesitate when giving money, and although I won't spend pages preaching why everyone must tithe, I will say that giving a part of your earnings is imperative. Mounds and mounds of Scripture support this.

As far as giving to other places and organizations, I think people are a bit cautious to jump into writing a check or handing out cash. I know I am. Before you can assist in any situation, you need to actually see a need. So the first step in being generous with money is to have the eyes and heart for a cause. Try the following:

In Your Home

- **If you don't have an allowance system in place, get to it.** Show your kids how to save so your kids can have something of their own to give.

- **Tell your kids where your money goes.** Discuss bills, but also tell them about where and why your family gives to the places you do.
- **Involve yourself in ministries you are already involved in.** If you sponsor a child, write the child. If you support missionaries, write to the missionaries. Help your kids see that involvement is about more than just a check.

In Your Community

- **Love bomb a neighbor.** My friend tells the story of over twenty-five people showing up at an unsuspecting neighbor's house. Unemployed for months, this neighbor needed much but asked for little. Instead of waiting, people brought boxes of nonperishables, health and beauty supplies, laundry detergent, diapers, and gift cards. Spend your money in the name of love. Love bomb. Who wouldn't feel loved? Have twenty-five people showed up at your house unexpectedly? Crazy!
- **Help fund a skate park.** Okay, so not really, but read up on local fundraising activities that interest you and, more importantly, interest your children. You may not be jazzed about raising funds for a skate park, but I bet your kid is.
- **Ask your pastor about specific needs he knows about but others do not.** Just because we don't know about a need doesn't mean it isn't there. Poke around a bit.

In The World

- **Buy fair trade products.** Make this site a favorite: http://fairtradeusa.org/products-partners
- **Educate yourself on your favorite charity's spending.** Research the ratings of both national and international organizations you support with Charity Navigator

(http://www.charitynavigator.org), American Institute of Philanthropy (http://www.charitywatch.org), or Better Business Bureau (http://www.bbb.org).

- **Give a microloan.** Microloans are very small loans (think $25.00) to people in poverty. If this is new to you, check out http://www.kiva.org.
- **Read.** *Toxic Charity* by Robert D. Lupton or *When Helping Hurts* by Brian Fikkert will make you re-evaluate not only the financial pieces of giving but also the big ideas about giving in general.

Dinner Table Dialogue

- Ask your family who they would like to help financially.
- How much should we give?
- Read Proverbs 3:9 together and discuss. *Honor the Lord with your wealth, with the first fruits of all your crops; then your barns will be filled to overflowing, and your vats will brim over with new wine.*

CHAPTER 10

THE CONCLUSION
But Not "The End"

My fifth-grade teacher, Mr. Munger, said you should never write the words, "The End." At the time, he referred to a crazy narrative I wrote about talking trees, but I think it applies here too.

Learning to fight selfish desires and serve others doesn't have an ending.

It's like loving someone: it starts out with a simple crush and grows into something you never expected. It makes you feel like dancing in the rain, and it digs holes in places of your heart you never knew existed.

I pray your family finds a person or cause that grabs ahold of your thoughts and that God chases you relentlessly until you decide to act. The only way we can show our kids the value of people is to humbly acknowledge we are all failing humans in desperate need of God (and each other).

If you dropped by our house, I wish I could say you'd find us prayer walking through our neighborhood or creating cards for residents at a local nursing home. But, if you stopped by our house, you would discover a selfish family. Just yesterday I faked sick to get out of an obligation. Nothing says "I'm here to help" like lying in bed watching back-to-back episodes of *The Tudors* on Netflix.

The day before, our youngest went nuts at Target because she wanted us to buy her a toy she already owned. It's okay (the guilt-free zone applies to me too).

Some days are like that.

When I feel as if there is no possible way our family can consistently put the needs of others above our own needs, I fall back on what Jesus said to the disciples when they questioned Him about how to enter God's Kingdom.

Jesus looked hard at them and said, "No chance at all if you think you can pull it off yourself. Every chance in the world if you trust God to do it." (Matthew 19:26, *The Message*)[1]

TO A DAD FROM A DAD

Dear Dads,

You may be reading this book on your own, or your lovely wife is "strongly" encouraging you to read it, but however you got here, welcome!

I wish I could write to you how gung-ho I was when our family decided to approach life with a more others-centered attitude, but that would be a lie. I am a creature of habit, and I like to live in the box.

When I first started thinking about how we lived life and about the changes I hoped to see in our family, I felt overwhelmed. I liked *my* time, and I'd worked hard to finally get *my* time the way I wanted it. However, as I reluctantly put my toe in the waters of change, I began to see the bigger picture.

For one, our oldest daughter was becoming a mirror of her dad. She loved *her* time and protected *her* time at all cost. This convicted me and reminded me how powerful our influence is as parents. We (parents) are the ones who set the tone and create the culture in our family.

Even though it was tough to get on board with this right away, I will tell you how deeply satisfying it is as a parent to see your children living an others-centered life.

Here are a few tips I have learned along the way:

- **Try being the mastermind behind some service opportunities.** I find that when I plan something, a natural outcome is I am more invested in what I'm doing.

When I don't plan it, I am at the mercy of something my wife and kids come up with (I can't explain how terrible the whole milk-carton-cutting craft incident mentioned in Chapter 2 was.).

- **Get involved in something you actually like**. I love projects, and I like to see what a final product looks like. So, cleaning up a section of riverfront or sprucing up someone's landscaping is in my wheelhouse.
- **Commit to create more than you consume**. When you live an others-centered life, you engage in activities that add to your world, such as building relationships, completing projects, creating memories, and learning from others. I have found when I am in full Me Mode, my mindset is very inward-focused and self-absorbed.
- **There's actually time for others and myself.** A big misconception I had when we started putting others first was that I would have zero time for things I enjoy, like sports. But that is not the case.
- **Pray.** Our family has learned serving others isn't about tasks. Pray God brings people and opportunities into your life, and He will.

Good luck.
Shane

BOOKS TO INSPIRE ACTION

Adults

Love Does: Discovering a Secretly Incredible Life in an Ordinary World, Bob Goff.
Just Do Something: A Liberating Approach to Finding God's Will, Kevin De Young.
Little Princes, Conor Grennan.
Same Kind of Different As Me: A Modern-Day Slave, An Art Dealer, and the Woman Who Bound Them Together, Ron Hall, Denver Moore, Lynn Vincent.
Rich Christians in the Age of Hunger, Ronald J. Sider.
Half the Sky: Turning Oppression into Opportunity for Women Worldwide, Nikolas D. Kristof and Sheryl WuDunn.
Growing Grateful Kids: Teaching Them to Appreciate an Extraordinary God in Ordinary Places, Susie Larson.
What Can I Do? Making a Global Difference Right Where You Are, David Livermore.
Small Things with Great Love: Adventures in Loving Your Neighbor, Margot Starbuck.

Kids

The Jesus Storybook Bible, Sally Lloyd-Jones.

What the World Eats, Photographs by Peter Menzel and Written by Faith D'Aluisio.

One Hen: How One Small Loan Made a Big Difference, Katie Smith Milway.

If the World Were a Village, David J. Smith.

Silver Packages, An Appalachian Christmas Story, Cynthia Rylant.

When Stories Fell Like Shooting Stars, Valiska Gregory.

Material World: A Global Family Portrait, Peter Menzel, Peter, Charles C. Mann, Paul M. Kennedy.

QUALITY TIME ACTIVITIES KIDS ACTUALLY WANT TO DO

Dear Parents,

If you go to unplugged days, you will have more time for other people. This means you will have more time for your kids, too.

I know you probably have some good ideas about fun things to do with your kids, but in case you need some more ideas, I made this list for you.

Love,
Amelia, age ten

1. Pretend you are robots.
2. Make forts out of blankets and chairs in your house.
3. Pick flowers from the yard and make a bouquet.
4. If it snows, make a snowman and dress it up like Taylor Swift.
5. Have a scavenger hunt.
6. Have a Make Your Own Pizza Night, and put peppers, cheese, and pepperoni on top of your little pizzas.
7. Ride your bike and look around for mushrooms.
8. Rent your favorite movie. Make a little bed on the living room floor. Pop popcorn, and then put salt, butter, and parmesan cheese on it.

9. Have a lemonade stand.
10. Create an obstacle course around your yard and time each other on it.
11. Hold a hula-hooping contest.
12. Have a picnic or tea party in your yard.
13. Teach each other jump rope tricks.
14. Draw self-portraits with sidewalk chalk.
15. Go to the pool. If you can, find an outdoor pool, and go there so you can see more nature.
16. Buy a puzzle with a lot of pieces and put it together.
17. Take the cushions off your couch and pretend it's a spaceship.
18. Plant a flower.
19. Paint your toenails like a beach ball. Make the colors go: purple, blue, pink, orange, and green.
20. Play hide and seek in the house or outside.
21. Read a book together, but pick an exciting book, and not a book about geography or a book that says something like, "Heather lived in 1943 and died in 1992. She did a lot of great things because she was a famous person."
22. Have a fire and make s'mores and hot dogs.
23. Go on a hike, but make sure there is something at the end of the hike to see, like a little pond or a waterfall.
24. Make a photo album.
25. Bake yellow cupcakes with chocolate frosting.
26. Plan a family talent show and make tickets for each person in the family.
27. Have a pretend daycare with all of your baby dolls and take the kids from the daycare on a field trip.
28. Make necklaces out of string and beads.
29. Hook up a hose and spray each other.
30. Make up a dance routine.
31. Collect rocks.
32. Take silly pictures of your feet or of a family member giving the evil eye.
33. Play tennis.
34. Go outside, look for birds, and count them.

35. Pitch a tent in the front yard and sleep in it.
36. If you have a sandbox, make a castle and pretend you live in it. If you don't have a sandbox, go to the park and look for one.
37. Ride bikes. If you have a little baby, someone could push him in a stroller, or you could put them in a bike trailer.
38. Make paper airplanes and try to throw them at each other.
39. Go to the library, but not too much.
40. Play catch in the yard.
41. Cut things out of paper. If you need an idea, you could do a hat or a hula skirt.
42. Get cards and play Go Fish, Crazy Eights, War, or Old Maid.
43. Make a time capsule. You could put important things in it like a dollar, a piece of candy that wouldn't melt, a pen, and a piece of paper. Then stick a note on it that says, "Don't open this until 2040."
44. Make a feeder for the birds. For example, string some popcorn.
45. Create a memory book out of a notebook, and write down funny stories that you remember from your day.
46. Make breakfast for dinner and serve waffles or chocolate chip pancakes.
47. Have a costume day, and dress up like a ghost or super hero.
48. Go outside and play tag or freeze tag.
49. Hold a family coloring contest.
50. Walk in your neighborhood and play I Spy.

31 DAYS OF GROWING GIVING HEARTS

A Prayer Calendar

Day 1: Remember Christ came to serve. Pray Mark 10:45.
Day 2: Give second chances. Pray Luke 17:4.
Day 3: Excel in giving. Pray 2 Corinthians 8:7.
Day 4: Love those you don't even like. Pray Romans 12:14.
Day 5: Encourage others. Pray 1 Thessalonians 5:11.
Day 6: Have a servant's heart. Pray Romans 12:11.
Day 7: Love greatly. Pray John 15:12.
Day 8: Show a genuine interest in others. Pray Philippians 2:4.
Day 9: Give your full attention. Pray James 1:19-20.
Day 10: Live what you know to be good. Pray Philippians 4:8-9.
Day 11: Ease another's burdens. Pray Galatians 4:14.
Day 12: Commit what you do to the Lord. Pray Proverbs 16:3.
Day 13: Invite friends over. Pray 1 Peter 4:9.
Day 14: Love actively. Pray Romans 12:9-13.
Day 15: Use kind words. Pray Ephesians 4:29.
Day 16: Pray continuously. Pray 1 Timothy 2:8.
Day 17: Remember those who suffer. Pray Hebrews 13:3.
Day 18: Share with others. Pray Romans 9:13.
Day 19: Show mercy. Pray Matthew 5:7.
Day 20: Act with patience. Pray Ephesians 4:2.

Day 21: Have courage. Pray Deuteronomy 31:6.
Day 22: Show patience. Pray Ephesians 4:2.
Day 23: Build people up. Pray Romans 15:2.
Day 24: Learn to listen. Pray James 1:19-20.
Day 25: Love your neighbor. Pray Matthew 22:39.
Day 26: Don't give up. Pray Colossians 1:1.
Day 27: Believe in miracles. Pray John 14:11.
Day 28: Forgive. Pray Hebrews 8:12.
Day 29: Conquer doubt. Pray Matthew 21:22.
Day 30: Overflow with hope. Pray Romans 15:13.
Day 31: Celebrate the power of the Gospel. Pray Luke 15:10.

CLICKETY, CLICK:
DOING GOOD ONLINE

Family-friendly websites, videos, and nonprofits:

http://www.onehen.org
http://www.storyofstuff.org
http://www.handsonnetwork.org
http://freerice.com/about
http://www.globalrichlist.com
http://www.dosomething.org/about/who-we-are
http://www.headbandsofhope.org
http://www.questforcompassion.org
http://www.unicefusa.org/campaigns/
http://www.bigheartedfamilies.org
http://www.crafthope.com
http://www.igive.com/welcome/lptest/cr40.cfm
http://ilikegiving.com
https://www.purecharity.com

Because of the ever-changing nature of the Internet, any web addresses or links listed in this book may have changed since publication and may no longer be valid.

CONNECT WITH AMY

I believe in a life that values people over possessions, others over us, and service over entitlement. My favorite stories of service involve quiet givers whose simple acts often remain unseen, but I'm also a sucker for the big, loud world-changers who passionately dart into the unknown. For some reason, I think you, dear reader, are a little bit of both.

I'd love to hear from you. I want you to tell me about all of the mischief you and your family get into as you attempt to serve others and our great, big God.

Connect with me at www.AmyLSullivan.com.

MY PORTION OF THIS BOOK'S PROCEEDS WILL GO HERE, ALL OF IT

After much prayer, the Sullivans have concluded all proceeds Amy receives from *When More is Not Enough – How to Stop Giving Your Kids What They Want and Give Them What They Need* will go toward the building of Asheville-Buncombe Community Christian Ministry's Transformation Village. Transformation Village will provide housing and job training programs for single women, women veterans, mothers with children, and intact families in crisis in Western North Carolina.

The Sullivans believe in the vision of Transformation Village and have personally witnessed it change lives. By purchasing this book, you are playing an important part in this process.

Good job, you!

High five!

For more information on Transformation Village, visit ABCCM online at http://www.abccm.org/transformation-village/

NOTES

Chapter 1: Battling the Beast We Helped Create

1. Campbell, W. Keith and Twenge, Jean M., *The Narcissism Epidemic: Living in the Age of Entitlement.* (New York, NY: Atria Paperback, 2009), p. 74.

2. Paul Davidson, "Managers to Millennials: Job Interview No Time to Text," *USA TODAY.com,* April 29, 2013, http://www.usatoday.com/story/money/business/2013/04/28/college-grads-job-interviews/2113505/.

3. "Reshini Premaratne's X-Out Homelessness", Generation One: Service Stories. May 18, 2013. http://www.generationon.org/service-stories/12642.

Chapter 4: Generous With Your Skills

1. Meltzer, Brad. *Heroes for my Son* (New York, New York: Harper 2010), 7.

2. Sims, Jade. Email interview July 15, 2013.

Chapter 5: Generous with Strangers

1. Seaton, Michael R. and Wiersma Ashley. *Start> Becoming a Good Samaritan.* DVD. (Grand Rapids, MI: Zondervan, 2009), Segment 1.

2. Alexander Peter, Lawrence. The Road of Blood. *The Untold Story Of The Good Samaritan.* (Petersburg, Virginia: Alexander Publishing 2008), p. 3.

3. Lawrence, Brother. *The Practice of the Presence of God.* (New Kensington, PA: Whitaker House, 1982), p. 21

4. Ibid., Segment 1.

5. Ibid., Segment 1.

Chapter 6: Generous with Forgiveness

1. "Amish School Shooting". Lancaster PA: Pennsylvania Dutch Country Welcome Center, http://www.800padutch.com/amish-shooting.shtml (accessed July 15, 2013).

2. Shaprio, Joseph. "Amish Forgive School Shooter, Struggle with Grief" from NPR's *All Things Considered.* http://www.npr.org/templates/story/story.php?storyId=14900930   (accessed July 15, 2013).

3. Mauriello, Tracie. "Amish Extend Hand to Family of School-house Killer" Pittsburgh Post Gazette, Post-Gazette.com Local, http://www.post-gazette.com/pg/06280/728083-85.stm   (accessed July 15, 2013).

4. Kraybill Donald, B., Noldt Steven M., and Weaver-Zercher David L. *Amish Grace: How Forgiveness Transcended Tragedy* (Jossey-Bass Books, San Francisco, California:1991), 68.

5. Ibid., 88.

6. The Forgiveness Project. Stories: Geoff Thompson (England) http://theforgivenessproject.com/stories/geoff-thompson-england/ (accessed July 15, 2013).

7. Nieder, John and Thompson, Tomas M. *Forgive and Love Again* (Eugene, Oregon: Harvest House, 1991), 63.

8. Ibid., 63.

Chapter 8: Generous with Prayer

1. Peterson, Eugene, Scripture take from THE MESSAGE. Copyright © 1993, 1994, 1995, 1996, 2000, 2001, 2002. Used with permission of NavPress Publishing Group.

Chapter 9: Generous with Money

1. Azim, Jamal and McKinnon Harvey, *The Power of Giving: How Giving Back Unites Us All* (New York, New York: Jeremy P. Tarcher/Penguin, 2009), p.79.

2. Peterson, Eugene, Scripture take from THE MESSAGE. Copyright © 1993, 1994, 1995, 1996, 2000, 2001, 2002. Used with permission of NavPress Publishing Group.

Made in the USA
San Bernardino, CA
29 September 2014